Many thanks to my good friend and professional peer - Francesca Douglas, for helping make this book a reality.

Marketing Skills Academy is a registered trading name for Elevation Marketing Limited. Registered in England & Wales No. 9163358.

Ordering Information: Quantity sales - special discounts are available on quantity purchases by corporations, associations, and others. For details, contact the publisher at the address above. Printed in the United Kingdom.

ISBN 978-1-3999-6651-1 (Paperback – first edition)

Cover and interior design by Mark Bland
www.getnoticedbranding.co.uk

Contents

Welcome 01

Introduction 08

What is Personal Branding? 12

Stage 1: PURPOSE 30

- Values..35
- Goals 36
- Actions...37

Stage 2: PERSONA 40

- Building credibility 42
- Create your Personal Branding Story 48
- Brand Identity..52

Stage 3: PEOPLE 54

- Defining your ideal customer.......................56
- How to define your niche.............................58
- Circle of Influence 65

Stage 4: PROPOSITION..**72**

- Unique Value Proposition (UVP)...74
- Monetising your proposition 77
- Authority Product 80

Stage 5: PROMOTION...**90**

- Personal brand ecosystem:
  - o Your website 93
  - o Social media 99
  - o Content 106
  - o Networking 118
  - o Recommendations / testimonials 124
  - o Email marketing 126
  - o Public Relations 131

**Bringing it all together: The role of
Perspective, Mindset, and Motivation** **136**

- Imposter Syndrome 139
- Mindset 143
- Self-reflection 146

Useful Resources **154**

About the Author...**176**

infectious
/ɪnˈfɛkʃəs/

adjective

Inspiring and radiating energy
in such a compelling manner
that it effortlessly resonates
with and motivates others
to embrace similar positive
sentiments and actions.

An undeniable influence
that spreads rapidly, leaving
an impactful and lasting
impression.

Welcome

If you are reading this book, then I shall assume that you are either:

1. Looking to market and grow within or on behalf of an existing business

2. Establish a reputable and effective brand presence on the market

3. Take your skillset and turn it in a new business venture

There has never been a better time for skilled professionals to proactively promote (and monetise) their experience, expertise, and industry presence – with the number of small business owners and self-employed individuals at an all-time high.

This book is going to walk you through six key steps that I believe are crucial when establishing your presence on the market. It's going to address five key areas of personal branding which cover that all important customer question: **WHY should I buy from THIS brand or individual?**

More than that, it's going to let you in on some secrets from deep inside the marketing industry, introducing you to concepts used by top brands to help them stand out and retain their position – but on a scale that is realistic for you as a smaller business owner or senior decision maker within an organisation. And it's going to do all that in a way which is understandable for regular people who aren't walking, talking marketing dictionaries.

That's right, no buzzwords, jargon, and convoluted explanations here!

So, before we begin, a little about me. After all – LESSON ONE – every prospective client, new customer, or person reading the foreword of a business book in the bookshop (hi reader!) wants to know one important thing first and foremost...

Why should they listen to you?

As a marketing and business consultant, my job is to work with entrepreneurs and business owners to finetune their offer, to define their place in the market, and to make sure that the audience they are reaching out to understands who they are and what they do.

Having worked in the marketing and brand communications sector for over 25 years, I have worked with a diverse range of public, private and third sector organisations. And while all of them have presented their own challenges, their own selling points, and their own added value, they each share one crucial thing...

"The most successful are the ones which are built on and rely on people, rather than systems and technology."

This book puts the spotlight on 'human-centred' organisations, and how celebrating the people in your business (including you) can not only give you an edge when it comes to branding but can enhance your competitor advantage and elevate your place in the market efficiently and effectively.

Who is this book for?

This book is packed full of marketing insight which bridges personal branding with the other key aspects of business marketing. It covers a full spectrum of marketing for the modern audience, stripping away the complexity of algorithms for different social platforms and how to "go viral" on TikTok – instead building the foundations of a truly future-proof marketing strategy for long term success.

As you read through this book, you will notice that I make regular references and notes for specific readers – namely the **entrepreneurs, solopreneurs,** and **intrapreneurs** among you.

So, which one are you?

Here are my three definitions for you to consider...

Solopreneurs

The term solopreneur has gained popularity in recent years due to the rise of the knowledge economy and the increasing number of people seeking independence and flexibility in their careers.

In simple terms, a solopreneur is an entrepreneur who operates their business alone, without the assistance of a team or employees. They are responsible for all aspects of their business, from ideation to execution and management – and might refer to themselves as self-employed or even freelance.

Solopreneurs typically leverage their skills and expertise to offer specialised services or products to a niche audience. While they may work alone, solopreneurs often collaborate with other professionals and contractors to grow their business and expand their reach – for example outsourcing particular aspects of work to other self-employed or freelance professionals.

Becoming a solopreneur is an exciting journey that offers independence, flexibility, and the opportunity to pursue one's passion. However, it's not for everyone. While anyone can become a solopreneur, it takes dedication, self-discipline, and a willingness to wear many hats. To run a successful 'solopreneurship', you must have a clear understanding of your skills, strengths, and goals. It's crucial to develop a strong brand identity and niche audience to differentiate yourself in the market – something that this book is going to shine a clear spotlight on.

Additionally, managing time effectively is crucial as you'll be responsible for all aspects of your business.

Remember, as a solopreneur, you are your own boss, and your success is entirely in your hands. With the right mindset, strategy, and hard work, you can achieve your goals and build a successful solopreneurship.

Entrepreneurs

An entrepreneur is an individual who creates, organises, and manages a business venture often with the aim of making a profit. They grow and develop teams of people to help pursue opportunities, utilising their innovative ideas, skills, and resources to create new products or services that meet market needs.

Entrepreneurs are driven by the desire to succeed, and they are not afraid to take calculated risks to achieve their goals. They are self-motivated, hardworking, and adaptable, able to navigate the challenges and uncertainties of the business world with resilience and determination.

Ultimately, entrepreneurs play a vital role in driving economic growth and innovation, creating jobs, and improving our quality of life.

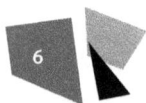

Intrapreneurs

An intrapreneur is an employee of an organisation who behaves like an entrepreneur, taking initiative and demonstrating innovative thinking and creative problem-solving skills. Intrapreneurs typically work within an existing company or organisation, using their entrepreneurial spirit to identify new opportunities, develop new products or services, or improve existing processes.

Intrapreneurs are not content with the status quo and are always looking for ways to add value to the company. Intrapreneurs often work collaboratively with others and are able to navigate complex organisational structures to achieve their goals.

Ultimately, entrepreneurship is a valuable asset to any organisation, as it fosters a culture of innovation and growth from within, with an intrapreneur someone who is employed by an existing business or company but infuses those skills within the workplace.

For intrapreneurs, this book is going to share insight into how to refine those skills for the benefit of both you and your workplace – separating your company from its competitors and giving you the insight and expertise needed to guide your company towards sustainable success.

Introduction

Since the global pandemic in 2020, millions of us have reassessed our relationship with work. After years of progressive change, mainly driven by the large global tech companies and some of the more 'switched-on' corporate organisations, there has been a growing realisation that the traditional 'work' model is potentially broken.

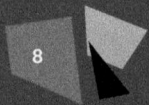

We no longer want our body clocks to be synced to the 9-5 treadmill, nor feel imprisoned in claustrophobic open plan offices. This has led to millions of us spending the past few years re-evaluating our work-life priorities. Some have switched careers. Others have opted for hybrid working, negotiated a reduction in hours or even decided upon early retirement. While others have chosen the more exciting and riskier option of self-employment.

One of the main reasons for the popularity of self-employment is the freedom and flexibility it offers. By working for yourself, you can set your own schedules, choose your own clients and projects, and work from anywhere in the world.

This level of autonomy is particularly appealing to those with specialised skills and knowledge, who may find that traditional employment arrangements don't allow them to fully utilise their expertise.

Technological advancements, changing attitudes and the growth of the gig economy are just a few of the factors driving this trend in which short-term contracts, freelance work, and on-demand services are the norm.

Hence, the rise of the 'knowledge economy', a term used to describe an economic system in which the primary source of value and growth is knowledge and ideas rather than physical goods. In this economy, the value of a company is determined not by its assets, but by its intellectual property and the expertise of its solopreneur founder and subsequent workforce.

In the knowledge economy, where expertise and knowledge are highly valued, having a strong personal brand can make all the difference. By establishing yourself as an expert, building a strong network, and being authentic, you can differentiate yourself from others and position yourself for success in this growing economy.

The knowledge economy is a reality, and having a clearly defined personal brand is essential for success in this new economic system.

But it doesn't end there – despite what other marketing books might have you believe.

You see, while many books and resources end with the design and construction of your personal brand, sending you off to merely add a quirky job title to your email signature or update your LinkedIn profile, I want to take this further by exploring how your personal brand impacts the various corners of your business model.

I'm going to share how your personal brand should be infused into the different touchpoints of your business, and how to make sure that you constantly connect your marketing to your audience through the power of personal branding.

Most of all, I want to teach you how to leverage your personal brand so that it connects you with the right people from day one – not just now but as your business grows, ensuring sustainable success.

But before we get there, we need to take yet another step back and consider the basics of your personal brand. **What is it, how do you create it, and why does it matter for entrepreneurs, solopreneurs, and intrapreneurs?**

Personal Branding...

What is it and why should I care?

The first thing I'm going to teach you about your personal brand is that you already have one – whether you are familiar with the concept or not.

Every working individual out there has some semblance of a personal brand – it's just that some are refined and deliberately constructed, while others are left to fend for themselves and are built from whatever they put out there.

Look at it this way. If your personal brand combines your interests and vision with your expertise, skills, and job role or business, then it follows that every piece of content you put out there to the wider world forms part of your personal branding.

Those that are aware of this will be working to make sure that everything they share fits together and supports their goals. Those who don't think about the connection between these elements are still constructing a personal brand; however, theirs is ineffective and confused, and could even stand in the way of future success if and when they try to change career or branch into a new business idea.

When harnessed correctly, your personal brand...

✓ **Has the power to grow your career** (or destroy it in seconds)

✓ **Is largely responsible for the working relationships you forge and your networking reputation**

✓ **Defines not only who you are, but how your business is run**

Most importantly, **your personal brand is the marketing tool on which the personality of an entire brand can be based** – whether you work for yourself, run an entire business, or act on behalf of an existing enterprise. When used correctly, your personal brand creates the base of an authentic brand which customers can grow to trust, that they will want to engage with, and that they will be happy to buy from. It sets the seeds for a good reputation, which positions your business as the solution to your customer's problems.

And that has never been more important than it is today.

As consumers, we are more highly brand-aware now than ever before, thanks to the plethora of brand advertising and promotional storytelling across our social media channels offering behind-the-scenes footage and insight across any and every industry. This is further compounded by the 24/7 access to daily news (and endless gossip) across a wide and diverse range of broadcast and editorial platforms.

Personal branding has the power to add a deeper story and outlook that is entirely separate from the business itself, but which becomes so closely intertwined with our business brand that the two are often associated as one and the same.

If you, as a business owner, want to stand out and be recognised as a thought leader or industry expert in an increasingly crowded and challenging marketplace, you must embrace the concept of personal branding and recognise how it can greatly benefit your business as a whole.

And it's not just business owners who can benefit!

For intrapreneurs, personal branding can be a way to establish yourself as an expert in your field of work within the business world, which can not only drive more clients and customers towards the company you work for, but which can set you in good stead for future opportunities.

Likewise for solopreneurs, the way you use personal branding becomes the very thing which draws clients to you rather than one of your competitors – singling out your vision and your expertise as the thing which sets you apart.

As you move through this book, you will find multiple references to personal branding for those who are solopreneurs as well as those who consider themselves to be intrapreneurial, potentially seeking a new challenge or taking on a new role as an employee within an organisation.

Because the simple fact is, personal branding is the way you associate and link your personality with your place in the business world - whether that be as an entrepreneur, intrapreneur or solopreneur, with tons of ideas just looking for a way to plant them.

Let's start with a definition of Personal Branding

Your personal brand is the means by which people remember you; with the term 'people' referring to your customer base, your business network, your colleagues and employees, and those who see your adverts and marketing campaigns. The people are, in essence, your audience.

This branding includes:

- ✓ who you are,
- ✓ what you stand for,
- ✓ how you present yourself – visually, emotively, and virtually

Visual Presentation: Personal branding involves how you visually represent yourself to others. This includes your physical appearance, grooming, style of clothing, and overall aesthetic. It emphasises the importance of creating a consistent and cohesive visual image that aligns with your personal brand.

Emotive Presentation: Personal branding goes beyond visuals and encompasses how you evoke emotions and perceptions in others. It focuses on expressing your values, personality, and unique qualities in ways that resonate with your target audience. This involves being authentic, genuine, and consistent in your interactions, communications, and behaviour.

Virtual Presentation: In today's digital age, personal branding extends to how you portray yourself online. It emphasises the way you present yourself through social media profiles, websites, and other digital platforms. It involves curating a strong online presence, including engaging content, professional images, and consistent messaging that aligns with your personal brand.

And it doesn't end there...

As well as presentation and the way others see you, your personal brand encapsulates a number of characteristics, including your knowledge, skills, expertise, achievements and the personality you inject into everything you do for and within your business.

It is a culmination of everything that your audience learns about you through your online presence and activity – which leads me onto a quick warning.

Whether you are an entrepreneur, intrapreneur or solopreneur, or just considering self-employment, you should be aware that everything you do will be perceived by your audience as part of your personal brand - whether or not it relates to your business.

Just like earlier when I touched on the fact that everyone has the start of a personal brand whether or not they know it, so too is it important to be aware that anything you do put out there, whether on your business account or not, is directly connected back to your personal brand and thus your business. This is because the higher and wider your exposure, the more your activity will be linked to your business, so be aware of what you are posting online and how you are interacting both now and with future growth and access in mind. It can and likely will be linked to your business at some point – even if not immediately – so make sure it supports that business and doesn't damage your image.

Why should we care about our personal brand?

Personal branding is 'personal and authentic'

'People buy from (authentic) people'.

Ever wondered why social media has become such a huge part of a successful digital marketing campaign, and why 'Stories' are the preferred means of posting? Because they are instant and present authentic insight into the behind-the-scenes life of a brand, business, or organisation.

Today's customers and consumers are more brand-aware and brand-educated than they have ever been before. Not only do they know your brand inside out, but they will also look to know as much as possible about you, your team, and the vision which motivates you.

As humans we are governed by our emotions. People want to buy from a brand that believes in and values the same things that they do, and it's your personal brand which adds a deeper story which becomes closely intertwined with your business brand.

To work, it needs to be personal to you and, above all, it must be authentic.

Personal branding builds authority

Authority builds trust. Trust builds relationships.

Relationships are what connect us to clients, customers, and opportunities within the business world and beyond.

Authority is not something we can freely or rightfully assign to ourselves; we must earn that recognition from our customers, colleagues, industry peers and employees.

Think for a moment about how often you have purchased from the same person or brand. They may not be the only one providing that product or service (or even the cheapest), but you chose them because of the relationship and trust you have personally developed with them – am I right?

Regardless of which industry or sector you operate in, whether you are a freelance service provider or work for a larger company, if potential customers feel they know you and believe that you can empathise with their pain points and provide an appropriate solution accordingly, they are more likely to engage with you and buy from you.

Moreover, when they engage with you – provided you offer a valuable interaction and product – they will inevitably draw more of their own network and other likeminded potential customers towards your brand.

Business branding can of course do some of the work here, as at the end of the day it is the business you want them to engage with rather than you, directly. But it's personal branding which will resonate most effectively and help customers and stakeholders to feel like they know you and want to buy personally from YOU (rather than your competitors).

Personal branding helps you stand out online

Most engagement and interaction between customers and businesses is now carried out online. The problem is that the online world has become an increasingly crowded environment, where algorithms and the vast selection of platforms make it difficult to find and entice the right audience.

So, how do you stand out from the crowd without relying constantly on gimmicks or big expensive campaigns?

Well, it all comes down to the way you inject personality and personal branding into the content and interactions that you share online.

Personal branding takes work and commitment but it's a powerful tool in your armoury, especially in the digital world. It can shape the way you use social media, can add extra weight to your marketing campaigns and launches, and can entice people into partnering with you as well as your business or brand. Make them like you, look out for you, and champion you above your competitors.

Personal branding allows you to build stronger contacts

Personal branding will help you build your professional network.

If your personal brand is strong enough, people will feel they know you; a benefit which carries over into your brand or business. They get what you stand for and find themselves drawn towards an alignment with your brand, it's values, beliefs and ideas – all because of what they see from and think about you as an individual.

More importantly, they see you as a trusted friend whose solution will genuinely support and help them – and others too.

This is where it becomes important to bridge personal with professional and ensure that everything you share online which is connected to your personal brand, is in line with your professional online presence. Remember that, particularly when you're an entrepreneur or solopreneur, everything you put out there is directly linked with your professional reputation, and so the messaging and vision you embody should complement your brand or business.

More on this, and how to establish and forge genuine connections and networks, later in this book.

Personal branding leads to more opportunities

There's no doubt that great personal branding delivers greater opportunities – no matter if you run your own business or work for someone else's.

If you are visible (and people like what you say or do), word of mouth and recommendations - particularly on social media - are likely to boost your appeal and your favourability rating.

This is **MARKETING GOLD DUST!** It's not **YOU** telling the world how awesome you are – it's **SOMEONE ELSE** – which can be incredibly powerful especially when it's fellow professionals, businesses, and customers words we trust most.

The benefit of enhanced opportunities for solo and entrepreneurs is obvious from a business perspective, but it's also a big one for intrapreneurs to focus on as this is where great connections for future roles and opportunities – both for you and the business you work for – can be built.

For example, you will notice that some Sales and Business Development professionals across different sectors all have excellent personal brands across their own accounts as well as their business profiles. This is because this one tool enables them to create connections and bring those connections in to generate opportunities for their company.

Personal branding isn't just for extroverts

Contrary to popular belief, you don't have to be an extrovert to build an effective personal brand. In fact, if you ask me, being an introvert is a personal branding superpower – and here's why.

As an introvert, you likely have skills that others don't have and that you can use to your advantage.

For example, introverted or less assertive individuals often excel in areas like listening, empathy, attention to detail, and thoughtful communication, which are all incredibly valuable skills, especially in today's increasingly interconnected world.

Using these skills as a core part of your personal brand, underpinning your entire business persona on your ability to listen with empathy and understanding, can become the thing that helps you to stand out.

Remember, the right clients will value the skills that you bring to the table, with my advice being to...

1. Embrace your unique skills and traits as an introverted professional (it doesn't make you any less knowledgeable, and it may make you more appealing than others to the right clients)

2. Focus on quality content that adds value

3. Leverage social media and establish an online presence that supports your business or place in the professional world

4. Attend smaller networking events and offer one-to-one sessions with clients for the more personal touch

5. Collaborate with others and let your skills and expertise shine, while bolstering your own perceived weaknesses with their strengths

In a world that often seems to favour extroversion - being an introvert is not a hindrance but a unique perspective!

With these tips, you can navigate, build, and promote your personal brand in a way that feels authentic and sustainable for you.

And with that in mind, let's talk weaknesses and how building a personal brand is a mechanism for overcoming real and perceived weaknesses in your business, career, or professional goals.

What are the main weaknesses that personal branding can overcome?

This is where the 3 C's come into play – **Clarity, Confidence, and Communication**.

These 3 C's embody three main weaknesses that solopreneurs and business professionals face but which personal branding can help to overcome. Again, this is not something which is exclusive to business owners; in fact, knowing about these challenges and how to overcome them can benefit business professionals on every step of the ladder.

1. **Clarity** when it comes to defining a professional 'identity'; and subsequently sharing the value and worth that you can offer to stakeholders such as your customers, employers, colleagues, peers and trade partners.

2. **Confidence** in demonstrating your abilities and core strengths to personal stakeholders, including customers especially.

3. **Communication skills** when it comes to articulating and sharing your ideas, opinions, vision and beliefs, in the most effective and efficient way possible.

When you don't have all three of these areas covered, your personal brand will suffer.

- Without **clarity** - what is your value?

- Without **confidence** - how can you expect others to feel confident in you?

- Without **communication** - how do you let others know about you and your truly unique personal brand?

Taking the time to consider and build a purposeful personal brand will inevitably take you on a journey towards deciphering not only what your value is as a professional, but what makes you stand out and how best to communicate this.

Whether on behalf of your own business or to meet goals in the workplace while finetuning your own industry position, connecting your personal brand back to the 3 C's will ensure that everything you put out there is consistently ticking these important boxes in the eyes of your customer.

Remember that
customers want CLEAR
solutions that they
can feel CONFIDENT
in, and which are
COMMUNICATED
effectively and efficiently.

It's now time to elevate your status to become a 5-P-Preneur

This is a book built on the concept of personal branding – aided by my own methodology – which invites you to ultimately take a step back and consider the connection between how you present yourself and how your brand or business is perceived.

By nurturing a refined personal brand online which depicts you in the way that you want your target audience and customers to see you, both you and your business or brand will gain the following...

Stage 1 **Purpose**

Passion · Values · Goals

Stage 2 **Persona**

Credibility · Story · Identity

Stage 3 **People**

Customers · Circle of Influence

Stage 4 **Proposition**

Unique Value Proposition
Monetisation · Authority Product

Stage 5 **Promotion**

Website · Social Media · Content
Networking · Recommendations
Email · Public Relations

This carries you from solo, entra, or intrapreneur to becoming a 5-P-Preneur, guided by the 5 P's which I believe tick all corners of a successful business model, regardless of where you sit in that model.

Crucially, it doesn't matter where you are starting from or what your end goal is. This book, and the methodology behind it, is designed to help any professional in any corner of the business world to refine their online presence and use it to generate success.

Whether you work as a freelance solopreneur, are taking the next step into launching a new business or want to strengthen your connections within an industry that you work in as an employee, personal branding and the 5 P's make you better at what you do.

And when you become better at what you do, you open new doors, create new opportunities, and ultimately future-proof your personal and professional success.

As you progress through this book, you will find yourself answering questions that seem unrelated to your business or your profession; but which can in fact prove invaluable in getting you to a place where WHO you are can truly benefit WHAT you do and WHAT you sell.

So, let's move into stage one: **Purpose**

Stage 1:
Purpose

'Purpose isn't a discovery; it's a creation. It's a journey of self-discovery and exploration, where we reflect on our values, passions, and strengths to shape our own destiny.'

Purpose is something that frames everything we do, every decision we make, and every road we take both in our business and professional lives, and in our personal lives. Yet, you wouldn't believe how many business professionals struggle to identify and communicate exactly what purpose drives them every day.

As part of your personal brand, being able to identify this fundamental reason behind what you are doing is key – not just in terms of motivating yourself every day, but with regards to what you offer to clients and customers, and why they should choose you. As a brand or business owner purpose becomes an integral part of your USP.

If you don't know what it is, how can you expect others to recognise it?

Your personal brand purpose model:

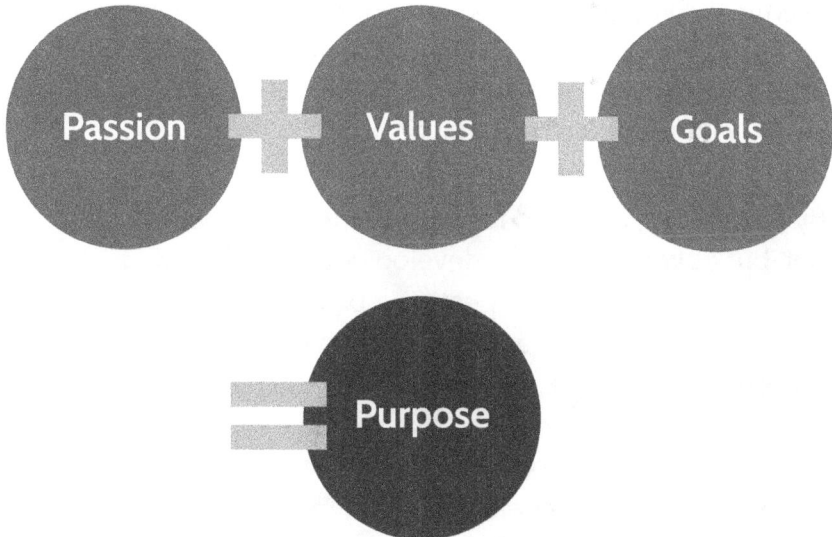

Passion + Values + Goals

= Purpose

So, what is your purpose?

As a coach and mentor for many entrepreneurs, intrapreneurs, and solopreneurs, one of the main issues I encounter regularly is the loss of purpose. That is, the purpose that once drove the individual has disintegrated.

This can happen for a number of reasons:

- They have reached a certain time in their career or life
- The 'dream career' they thought they were striving to achieve, has not worked out as planned
- They have accomplished or exceeded their goals
- Relationships or family circumstances have changed (I often hear 'our children have flown the nest' or 'I'm no longer with my partner – and need to move on, I need a new challenge!')

Suddenly, even those running successful businesses and seemingly hitting all their goals find themselves feeling lost, confused, demotivated, lonely, and fearful for the future.

How do we change this?

By recognising the need for purpose not just when we start out, but as we continue to develop both ourselves and our business. You wouldn't expect your business targets to be the same year on year as you grow, so why should your personal and business purpose remain stagnant? Growing and developing is something that should be reflected in your purpose and motivation – with the most successful business people updating their personal brand regularly to reflect where they are in the here and now.

However, there are parts of this that resonate differently with different people – and the way that you run your business or shape your professional life can play a major role in your purpose.

Purpose is not something that we discover, but rather something that we create. It is a process of self-discovery and exploration that requires us to reflect on our values, passions, and strengths.

> As a **solopreneur**, purpose will always play an integral role - not only in WHAT you do, but WHY you do it – and HOW you do it.

> Similarly, **entrepreneurs** build entire businesses on their own purpose and what motivates and drives them – believing strongly in an idea which resonates with them.

> For those **intrapreneurs** who work for others while infusing their own ideas and vision into their role, purpose can often be confused with the vision of the business that you work for – with intrapreneurs needing to balance their own purpose with that of their employer.

For me, my purpose lies in supporting and educating others as they find their WHY and HOW.

I believe in helping people like you solve the fundamental challenges they have in defining what their business solution is and how it supports people - and by working with individual and large business teams, I motivate and help them to understand what they are selling, how, and who to.

That's my purpose – and it's reflected not just in my business model but in every communication and message I put out there.

If you're struggling to find your purpose – one place to start is with another 'p': Passion.

The role of Passion

Understanding your purpose means thinking about your own WHY. That is, why are you doing what you are doing?

For most of us, that starts with a passion – be it for a better work-life balance, a specific job role, or a passion that we transform into a business.

In order to determine where your passion lies and thus what your purpose should be built on, start by answering these questions...

- ✓ What are you passionate about, interested and experienced in?
- ✓ What are the things in life which interest you, and which you look to pursue at every available opportunity?
- ✓ What motivates you?
- ✓ How can you turn that motivation into a career or business idea?

As you answer these questions, look for patterns. What activities or experiences have brought you the most joy and fulfilment? Are your passions directly linked to your professional life, or do you operate on more of a 'work to live' basis?

Ultimately, by answering these questions and considering where your passion lies, this section will introduce you to three core areas of your business persona which become a part of the foundation for your purpose and thus your personal brand. These three areas are:

1. Values
2. Goals
3. Actions

Via these three areas of focus, your purpose becomes part of your brand or business persona – ultimately connecting you with the demographic that you consider to be your core audience. Let's take a closer look at how all three of these contribute towards the creation of your purpose, and how it all comes together as one of the crucial 5-P's.

Values

Values are the fundamental reasons for why you do what you do, why you do it, and why you want to do it. We all have them, and live our lives by them, but each of us have a different set of values based on our social upbringing, cultural influences, moral teachings and life experiences.

And it's not just in our personal lives.

Values are at the heart of our personal brand too. They dictate, often subconsciously, how we communicate and interact with other people – in our work as well as personal lives.

As humans, we tend to feel closer to, and relate more with, people who share similar values to ours, and this can be an important aspect to focus on when developing a personal brand.

Consider what your values are and how important they are to your professional life:

- What do you believe in – morally, ethically, even spiritually? Do you have a certain way you conduct relationships, especially in business?
- How do your values influence your behaviours, actions and decisions, especially in a professional environment?
- How do your values motivate you – do they provide guidelines and boundaries? Do they stimulate ambition and achievement?

Goals

This is where it becomes a little more focused on you. **If your Values are the why**, then **Goals are what, how, and when** – and are backed up by point three: **your Actions**.

Your goals should set the desired direction in which your personal brand will be positioned, so that you can align your business with your value, or bring extra value into your role within a team or a company. Thus is where you need to really step back and consider how you want your personal brand to impact your professional standing.

- Beliefs — WHAT do you believe you could achieve with your personal brand?

- For example...
  - Become a thought leader in your industry — inspire others or motivate change
  - A new job — a new challenge / development opportunity
  - Launch your own business (or side hustle) — sell your skills, passion and expertise
  - Achieve a promotion with your current employer — increase in salary and responsibility
  - Get involved with or create a charitable venture that addresses social or humanitarian needs
  - Other...

Actions

When you combine your values with your goals, you can start to identify the best course of action — that is, what you need to do in order to reach those goals while upholding your values.

For many clients I work with, the best way to set a standard for action is by creating a timeline with set deadlines under which certain goals will be met.

For example, if the end goal is to launch a new online course within two months, the actions you take should be geared towards this while tapping into the values which connect you with your ideal groups of guests.

If your ideal guests are young families, then use your own values to connect and engage with these people and take action in introducing and launching your course concept to them, in time for the big launch.

As you start to build these three core areas of your business, you will find yourself with the foundations of a personal brand centred on Purpose.

The Why, the What, and the How

- Belief
- Intention
- Action
- Result

Make it work for you...

For solopreneurs:

- *Purpose will help you identify what area of expertise or service to operate in.*
- *Combine your values with your purpose, and use that as part of your networking to meet and connect with clients and customers.*
- *Purpose will help you on tough days, and will remind you of what motivates you.*

For entrepreneurs:

- *Purpose forms an integral part of your brand or company vision and mission statement and should be seen as the Bible of your company marketing.*
- *Purpose connects you as an entrepreneur with the brand or company you have created. Use it to ground you when pitching or presenting.*

For intrapreneurs:

- *Make sure that everything you do within your role is connected to an overarching purpose.*
- *Take care not to allow your purpose to be diluted by company goals and the vision of your boss or manager.*
- *Try to work in harmony.*

Stage 2:
Persona

'If Purpose looks at WHY you do what you do, then Persona deals with the question on every customer's lips: Why should I trust YOU?'

Your persona is the way that others view and perceive you. This covers your presentation not just as an influencer in your field, but as a colleague, an employer, an employee, and even a friend.

For **solopreneurs**, it forms the foundation of long-term success and is the reason why clients will continue to come to you to access your expertise.

For **entrepreneurs**, it sets the standard for your company or brand, grounding it in reliable expertise under the name of its founder.

For **intrapreneurs**, it is the reason why colleagues trust you, why managers promote you, and even why customers choose your company over competitors.

So, to utilise persona in all its glory, you must ask yourself how to establish authority and credibility.

How do you create and establish trust in yourself as a brand and in your own personal ability – and most importantly, how do the two connect to make you a reliable go-to in your field?

Your personal brand persona model:

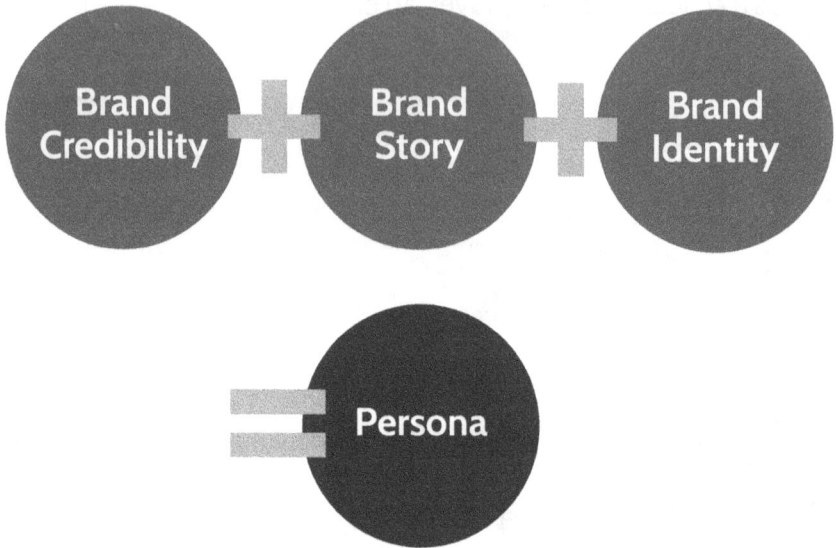

Brand Credibility + Brand Story + Brand Identity

= Persona

Building credibility through your experience, skills, and expertise

This is the part of your personal brand where I encourage you to think about why you are where you are, and what it is that makes you the best.

This is not the time to be coy about your experience and skillset, nor your achievements and little (and big) wins. It's also not the time to downplay your personality and the quirks that make you who you are. All of these things are crucial in establishing a persona that others can trust and that they will be drawn to.

By establishing the value of what you have done so far in terms of personal experiences and within your career, you immediately start to create links between your business persona and the small quirks and personality factors which make you, you.

The more links you can create between your business and your own personality, the easier your personal brand will be to finetune and bring to life in an authentic way.

Let's start with experience.

Experience

This is the most important point for many people as it establishes exactly why you are working in the sector you are in – whether as an employee or as a business owner or freelance solopreneur.

For potential clients or customers, experience is what lets them know that you understand the sector, that you know what you are talking about, and that you can provide them with the solution they need to a challenge or issue they are experiencing.

Some of the questions to ask yourself include:

What professional experience do you possess?

Intrapreneurs will find these skills invaluable to dissect and understand when it comes to applying for new roles, expanding within an existing role, or taking on new responsibility.

An ability to recognise your professional value and experience will help you to create compelling arguments for workplace development, promotion, and more.

Work:

- Jobs you have held, employed by someone else
- Jobs you have undertaken while self employed
- Secondments and other work-related experiences
- None Executive Director roles
- Professional societies / memberships / accreditations and awards

Leisure:

- Groups
- Societies
- Clubs
- Memberships

Voluntary:

- Charity work
- Community work
- Advisory or consultancy work

What **social skills** do you possess?

Social skills are the tools we use to communicate and interact with people, which can be verbal, nonverbal, written or visual. These skills are used by all different types of 'preneur', though are especially important for entrepreneurs who use social skills to pass their vision and business goals and ideas onto others.

Good communication relies on excellent social skills, with entrepreneurs finding that the entire success of a business could well rely on your ability to communicate your vision.

For example:

- Motivation
- Organisation
- Decision making
- Engaging
- Empathetic
- Positivity
- Delegation

What **personal skills** do you possess?

Personal skills are often referred to as 'soft' skills or 'people' skills.

Solopreneurs tend to find these personal skills to be especially critical, as they are what enable you to maintain and nurture positive relationships with clients.

For example:

- Communication
- Negotiation
- Leadership
- Interpersonal
- Critical thinking
- Time management
- Presentation

Expertise

Once you have defined your various experiences, it's time to work out which skills link those experiences and, crucially, which skills can be defined under your own areas of 'expertise'.

Expertise covers those things that you consider yourself a master in, whether it be something you do for someone else, something you know a lot about, or something you can advise on. Solopreneurs should be particularly attuned to this as it likely forms the basis of their entire business or career.

For example:

- **I write** reports / strategic plans / articles / stories...
- **I build** products / experiences / environments...
- **I manage** processes / systems / procedures...
- **I create** graphics / videos / presentations / specifications...
- **I design** concepts / plans / blueprints / systems...
- **I teach** children / adults
- **I coach / train / mentor** individuals / teams / organisations...
- **I present** and / or facilitate meetings / seminars / speeches...
- **I conduct** interviews / assessments / mediations...
- **I organise** schedules / events / conferences...

Achievements

An achievement refers to something that you have been recognised for in a positive way. This doesn't have to be something you've received an award for - achievements can be much more 'everyday' than that (I call them the "little wins" – which can be just as important as the "big wins").

Ask yourself what you have achieved **successfully** using effort, skill, or courage.

For example:

- Education
- Career – being employed by someone else
- Career – being self employed
- Personal interests – clubs / societies / leisure pursuits
- Voluntary or charity work

These achievements can be used to great effect in your backstory, within an online profile, or even as part of the founding story for a new brand. Not only do they further support your expertise within a certain industry, but they add to the personality that modern customers want to find within your business – be it large or small.

Create your
Personal Brand
Story

This is the part of the book where we start to build on all those touchpoints that led to where you are now. The chances are that what you are doing at the moment, or what you are seeking to do with the help of this book, is based around the experiences you have, the expertise you've finessed, and the vision that drives you. Now it's time for all of that inner motivation to be shaped and finetuned as part of your personal branding story – the thing that celebrates who you are, what you are doing, and why you are doing it.

Let's be real for a minute.

We live in a crowded world with a plethora of influencers, commentators, and opinion leaders, all proactively promoting their beliefs and gaining followers in return. One of our biggest challenges is to break through the noise and establish our own place in the world - authentically, effectively, and successfully.

With the rapid growth of social media and other digital communications tools at our fingertips, we (and in turn our consumers) have become incredibly perceptive to fake, inauthentic and insincere business brands, which promote one thing and yet behave completely differently. We can, in short, spot them a mile off, and this also applies to people – celebrities, personalities, politicians and other people in the public eye.

Our 'BS-radar' can sense when someone is not being authentic, or when someone's story feels a little too good to be true – and the reality is that this falsehood puts us off instantly.

In fact, when you really think about it, it's not just about turning others off - it's also much more difficult keeping up a false pretence than it is simply being unapologetically and authentically 'you'.

So, how do we promote our 'authentic self' and cut through the noise in a way that is memorable and will actually attract the interest of people, while also ensuring that they recognise our value, trust in our experience, and view us as overtly reliable?

By telling people our story!

Stories can be engaging, enlightening and educational - some ticking just one of those boxes, while others tick all three.

Stories can also take us to another place, can enable us to gain new perspective, and can help us to understand things differently. And from a customer or client standpoint, stories can help them to make sense of what we as entrepreneurs or solopreneurs are offering – giving them the crucial WHY that makes the WHAT make sense.

In short, storytelling is a powerful technique which can bring together our business marketing and our personal brand - communicating our reasons for creating the business, for entering a specific industry, or for designing something new for the market.

It can be used to craft key messages and make them more attractive to a specific audience, capturing their attention and finding ways of building positive relationships with that audience.

That story begins here.

Utilising storytelling techniques to enhance your personal brand

Describe your journey

- How you arrived here. This may include your **career highlights** - how you have gained specific knowledge, skills and expertise; opportunities which you have experienced and excelled at!

- People you have worked with and interacted with – inspiring employers, amazing customers, great colleagues and peers... it could even be those who have been negative towards you but have helped you to grow!

- Do you have any specific anecdotes, narratives or recollections which can enhance the validity and understanding of your story?

- What lies ahead? What do you think may happen next? Let people in on what the future holds, and make them feel like a valued part of your journey.

Of course, all good stories need moments of adversity or obstacles to conquer

- Consider the challenges you have faced and how you have overcome them. How have you triumphed in the face of adversity? How has the negative insight of others helped to shape who you are - and what your business looks like - today?

- What lessons have you learned from these experiences – whether positive or negative - which could influence and help others.

For intrapreneurs especially, there's a reason why job interviews always touch on challenges you have experienced and ask for specific examples of how you overcame them. A great deal of your persona lies in your attitude and response to specific situations both personally and professionally, so the more you can do to work this into your personal brand the better.

Brand Identity

The final element of your Personal Brand's Persona is your brand identity. This contains the tangible and intangible elements which are based on your personality, presentation, and the way others perceive you – and should form an integral part of your presence online, across social media, and in everyday communications and interactions.

Have you ever noticed how some brands shroud all their social posts in innuendo and humour, while others take on a more emotive approach and strive to connect consumers to a problem and solution?

For example, if you're a solopreneur then you might start out with a personal social profile which you gradually build into a supporting platform for your brand – demonstrating how closely linked the two are while at the same time creating a bridge between you as a person and a supplier or service provider. This is one of the easiest ways to get started in building a brand identify with some semblance of an existing audience – not to mention, it gives you the boost of support you need from personal connections.

Make it work for you...

For solopreneurs:

- *Persona sets you apart from the competition, enabling clients to connect with you and view you as an expert that they trust and want to engage with.*
- *Use your professional profile to highlight your persona early on, and rely on reviews and the experiences of former and existing clients to really reinstate what puts you at the top of your game or industry.*
- *Think about the way you inject your professional brand identity into your communications, both online and via direct methods. It can be visual as well, in the name you use as your professional identity, and the images you share.*

For entrepreneurs:

- *Use persona as the foundation for your brand story, and ensure that every touchpoint and marketing campaign you release is directly reminiscent of that persona.*
- *The persona you share has a direct impact on the customers you draw in.*
- *Is there a way of using colour, visuals, and messaging to shape your persona? This is what we call 'physical brand identity' and is what will help customers to connect different content streams back to your brand or business.*

For intrapreneurs:

- *Persona plays a major role in how you are viewed as a colleague and employee, as well as an industry expert — and can impact your future career growth and development within a role.*
- *When you establish credibility in what you are saying, you ground the whole business or company in that same credibility and present yourself as a valuable asset.*

Stage 3:
People

When you know who your target audience is, you know who you are reaching out to, who you are talking to, and who you are trying to connect and network with.

If you want to create a successful brand which is renowned for delivering solutions to a captive audience, you need to understand not only who sits in that audience but what they think, what they need, what matters to them, and what they want from a brand or supplier. The business owners with the best personal brands are not those who are best able to communicate their own vision and motivation, but those who are able to align themselves with the people that matter most to them – their customers.

These are the professionals who channel just as much time (if not more) into growing and nurturing their target audience, as they do in building a cohesive marketing plan. They know who they are talking to, they know the value that each individual in their network presents, and they know how to harness that value for maximum effectiveness – all before they generate and share a single campaign or marketing post.

Understanding your target audience enables you to identify the individuals you are reaching out to, the people you are communicating with, and the connections you are trying to make and foster. And this is true whether you're doing it on behalf of a wider business as an entrepreneur, building your freelance connections as a solopreneur, or working under the umbrella of a business employer.

Your personal brand people model:

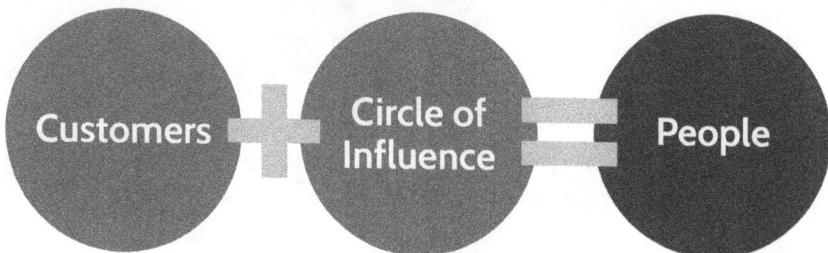

Customers + Circle of Influence = People

Knowing exactly who you're speaking to shapes everything from your own tone of voice in copy, to your marketing campaigns, the platforms you use, and the way you sell your products or services.

Defining your ideal customer

Now before we go any further, it's essential to understand one of the hardest truths of the business world – **not everyone is, or will become, your customer.**

It's surprising how many businesses are spreading themselves far too thin – wasting time, resources and money trying to market and sell to everyone.

As a **solopreneur**, it can be tempting to try to appeal to as many people as possible. After all, the more potential clients you can reach, the better, right?

Likewise, as an **entrepreneur**, especially one managing a new business opportunity, being too niche can feel like an unnecessary limiting factor in your business growth.

And, for those **intrapreneurs** building connections as part of their job, surely the best approach to personal branding and professional growth is to try and become what everyone needs – right?

Wrong!

The reality is that trying to market to everyone is a recipe for mediocre results and frustration. It creates a precedent which is impossible to keep up in the long run, as building and expanding a company, freelance business, or even the parameters of a job role naturally requires you to become more selective with regards to what you take on. You cannot build a business or professional empire and be what everyone needs, at all times.

So, you must carve out your business niche – and you must do it early on in your professional journey, using it to build a personal brand which organically connects you to your target audience and to your people.

Finding your market niche is, in the simplest sense, much more effective than trying to market to everyone. When you narrow down your focus to a specific group of people with a specific set of needs, you become much more valuable to them. You can tailor your services and skills to their unique challenges and pain points, and position yourself as an expert in your field.

Not only that, but when you have a specific market niche, you're much more likely to attract the kind of clients and customers who are the best fit for your services. These are the clients who will be most likely to benefit from your expertise, and who will be the most satisfied with the results.

How to define your niche

Here are some steps you can take to define your niche target market in a conversational tone:

1. Define your ideal customer/s

Ask yourself questions like:

- Who needs my product or service?
- What problems do they have that my product or service solves?
- What do they value?
- What specific skills do I have that I can bring to a job role, which colleagues and customers alike look for in my industry?

The questions that you ask at this early stage will of course vary depending on your professional position – whether you're building a company, finetuning your offer as a freelance solopreneur, or looking for clarity on how you specifically can add value to the business world through various roles and connections. However, the aim of this exercise remains the same – encouraging you to identify the defining features of the customers, clients, and even colleagues that you want to surround yourself with and work with.

2. Conduct some market research

Use social media, surveys, and other methods to gather information about your potential customers. This will help you understand their behaviours, preferences, and pain points. During this stage of the process, it is vital that you also spend time analysing your competition and determining how you can differentiate your business from theirs.

This will help you identify gaps in the market that you can fill. Again, the way you do this will depend on your professional position and what you are trying to achieve:

For **solopreneurs**, use this stage to identify the services that competitors offer and then consider factors like pricing, quality, service packages, and specific niche skills that make you stand out.

For **entrepreneurs**, this step of your journey is all about defining your USP and where your business fits in the broader industry and on the wider market. The chances are that you already know the pain points of your ideal customer – now it's time to take a step back and fill in some of the blanks about who those customers are and what motivates them.

For **intrapreneurs**, this is a two-pronged process as I encourage you to consider the people that matter to your professional position in terms of both customers and colleagues. In many ways, your personal brand is the most difficult to define because you're creating a persona that's good for the overall business you work for, attracting customers and inspiring and appealing to colleagues. Take this opportunity to work out the ideal people for your business and for you as an individual to appeal to.

3. Create a customer avatar

This is a fictional representation of your ideal customer, based on the above research. The chances are, you'll have a wide variety of people buying from you – and you'll never be able to identify and appeal to all of them.

However, having a basic idea of who you're speaking to and what has motivated them to come seeking your business or services can inform everything from the tone of your marketing to the packages and future products you create.

Use the following guide as a template to create a customer avatar for each type of customer (and consumer).

- **AVATAR NAME**
  A fictional name for this customer persona group

- **DEMOGRAPHICS**

  Who are they?
  (Individual / organisation / couple / group)
  What is their gender?
  (Male or female)
  How old are they?
  Age bracket (16–24; 25–34; 35–49; 50–64; 65+)
  What is their status / title?
  (Owner / MD, Director, Manager, Self-Employed, Retired...)

- **INTERESTS**

  What are their interests?
  (Sport, lifestyle, leisure, hobbies...)
  What are their likes and dislikes?

- **MEDIA CONSUMPTION**

  What is their media consumption?
  (Social media, websites, print, TV, radio)

  This question might seem random, but it is especially helpful when it comes to identifying innovative marketing opportunities - so don't skip it!

- **ROLES & RESPONSIBILITIES**
  (IF BUSINESS-TO-BUSINESS i.e., you are marketing and selling your products and services to other businesses)

  What type of business do they operate in?
  What is their main role?
  What are they responsible for?
  Are they a key decision maker for your product / service?
  What are their individual goals / objectives?

- **BUYING CYCLE**

  How often do they buy your product / service?
  (Hourly, daily, weekly, monthly, annually or infrequent)
  What is their average spend?
  (Per day / per week / per month / per year – choose which is the most applicable)
  Is price a decision factor for them when purchasing your product / service?
  Where do they purchase?
  (Online, telephone, instore or face-to-face)
  Are they loyal to you or do they shop around?

• PAIN POINTS

Part of defining the customer avatar involves identifying pain points.

These are problems or challenges that the customer experiences that may affect their buying decisions. Once you understand what pain points are, you can work out your response and increase the likelihood of the customer buying from your business.

When considering your marketing, addressing the pain points you identified is crucial – in essence, selling them the solution to a problem that you know they have.

Your competitors may have similar solutions to the same problems. How does your business go the extra mile?

What would make them feel special?

This is where you consider the parts of your business model which enable you to go the extra mile – whether as a business owner, a freelance service provider, or an employee.

> For **solopreneurs**, this is where connection and personality becomes a major part of your armoury – elevating your proposition over competitors through the way you engage with your clients, and through the services you offer them. You have the flexibility to work according to your own priorities, granting you the opportunity to over-deliver and give clients that buzz that will make them come back and keep choosing you.

For **entrepreneurs**, making customers feel special and valued should be a core part of your marketing focus – achievable through special offers and discounts, exclusive launches, and more. The way you communicate these will depend on your demographic and where your target customers engage with you, with social media and email marketing a good place to start.

For **intrapreneurs**, opportunities here can be limited – however, being able to offer different upgrades and uplifts to customer experiences can make them feel special and benefit the business through retention and customer loyalty. From the perspective of your position as an employee or colleague, it reflects what you bring to your team and how you go the extra mile for the business.

4. Test your assumptions by reaching out to your target market

Gather feedback on your messaging, branding, and product offerings. Use this feedback to refine your approach and make adjustments as needed.

Remember, your niche target market may change as your business evolves. Stay open to new ideas and be willing to adjust your strategy as needed.

By following these steps, you can define your niche target market and build a business that meets their needs and exceeds their expectations.

Find your customers

Now you know who your ideal niche customers are, it's time to find them. And I'll warn you now - with more social media channels and digital touchpoints available now than ever before, finding out where your customers hang out online, and cutting through the noise to reach them, is not easy.

The best place to start is with experimentation, identifying a handful of channels that you know are frequented by your core customer group, working out which ones garner the most engagement, and which ones work best for you and your business.

From there, it's all about using that personal brand we keep talking about, to reach out to and engage with the people who could become customers with the right nurture techniques.

Use your brand identity and the story we created in the previous chapter as a starting point, connecting yourself with the industry in which your customers operate and identifying yourself as a solution to problems they may have. This is something that you can do as an entrepreneur, intrapreneur, or solopreneur – leaning on your personal brand as the foundation on which customers connections are built for you and for your company or business.

Again, trial and error is an unavoidable part of this – and you will likely find that it takes time to establish a positive and trustworthy reputation. However, consistency is key.

Your Circle of Influence

Now that you have defined your ideal customer and worked out where to find them, the next stage is to consider your wider network (or as I like to call it - your Circle of Influence).

This is how you define your target audience – that is, all the people who are and could be influential to your personal brand.

Note how here I am referring to your target audience rather than your target customer. These terms are so often used interchangeably in the world of digital marketing; however, they couldn't be more different.

Your target customer is who you are looking to do business with. You engage with them with a very specific target and goal in mind, with conversion underpinning every conversation and interaction.

Whereas, your target audience refers to a much broader group which combines customers with everyone else who forms part of your professional network.

This network which makes up your target audience includes trusted colleagues and peers; suppliers and trade partners; competitors; local and regional community; regional and national media; political and business leaders; highly influential personalities in your industry; influencers and celebrities; even coaches and other business connections.

So, why do all these individuals and groups of people matter so much?

When you tap into your Circle of Influence, you begin to establish and build that credibility we've been talking so much about. Remember that old adage 'it's not what you know but who you know'? Well, this is crucial when it comes to personal branding and creating a position of trust and reliability in your chosen industry.

Introducing your Circle of Influence...

There are four levels of focus when it comes to your Circle of Influence. By applying this model to your target audience, you can gain a clear understanding of who lies at the heart of your personal brand, and how your circle can and should expand outwards as you invite more and more individuals into the fold. They may even be some cross-over e.g. a brand ambassador is also one of your decision makers...

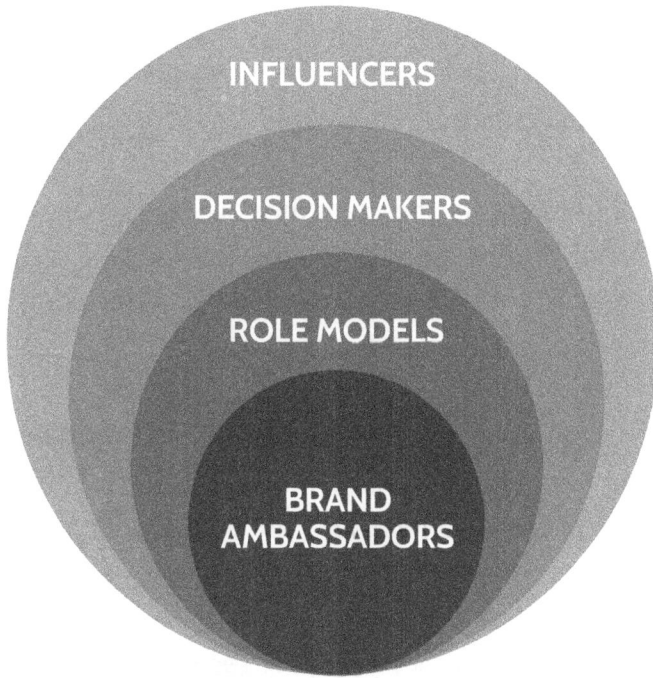

The diagram shows concentric circles labeled from outer to inner:
INFLUENCERS
DECISION MAKERS
ROLE MODELS
BRAND AMBASSADORS

1. **Identify your brand ambassadors** – at the very heart of your Circle of Influence are your brand ambassadors. These are the people who know, like and trust you and will speak highly of you. This could be customers, suppliers, colleagues, peers or even competitors!

   I would recommend choosing at least 6-9 people for this level.

2. **Identify your role models** – next are your role models, the people who inspire you, keep you focused and motivated. This may include other business owners / entrepreneurs, a business mentor or even your boss!

   I would recommend choosing at least 2-4 people for this level.

3. **Identify your decision makers** – this is an interesting category because who these people are and the role they play very much depends on your position.

   For entrepreneurs, these are the colleagues that you trust the most in your business – with access to business finances and the ability to make different decisions which affect operations, spend, goals, and more.

   For solopreneurs, your decision makers are a mixed bunch of clients and professional contacts, as well as those peers who directly support you and who influence major decisions you make that relate to your business goals.

   For intrapreneurs, these are your senior decision makers and any other major players whose own roles control and influence your position and the job you do on a daily basis.

   I would recommend choosing at least 3-5 people for this level, depending on your professional position.

4. **Identify your influencers** – finally, there are those people who are top of their game and well connected with a substantial network. They carry much influence and could accelerate your reach and business profile as well as introduce you to other notable influencers leading to new opportunities – provided you can connect to them!

   I would recommend choosing at least 2-3 people for this level.

Once you have your Circle of Influence established, it's time to consider the role that each person directly plays in your business – whether they are a valued colleague who sits beside you and facilitates everyday tasks you perform as part of your role, a client who always shares great reviews and has become a loyal repeat customer, or an influencer in your industry whose support can help you to reach a new audience.

You might find that some connections are not needed right away - in fact, as an initial step you probably only need ambassadors and a basic idea as to who your role models are. However, as you grow and start to establish your personal brand and thus your professional presence more clearly, reaching out to influencers for collaborations and introductions will give your personal brand - and your business - the weight it needs to move up a level in the game we call "business".

Ultimately, you will end up with a circle of individuals at different levels, each of whom can speak to a different aspect of working with you. Not only will this help you when it comes to marketing your business to customers; it will also help you when it comes to recruitment and hiring, partnerships, business growth, and industry collaborations.

Make it work for you...

For entrepreneurs:

- *Your people are your customers and those who work as part of your business, as well as those in the industry who inspire and challenge you in equal measure.*
- *Knowing who your customers are enables you to find them, connect with them, and position yourself and your brand as a solution to their problems.*
- *The better you know the people you're reaching out, the better able you are to create a personal brand which resonates with them.*

For intrapreneurs:

- *The people that matter are your colleagues at work, the customers that your company markets and sells to, and the connections which grant you opportunities for professional development inside and outside the workplace.*
- *Nurturing a personal brand which connects you to clients and customers is good for business, and helps you to become directly linked with expertise and knowledge which is beneficial to your development in the workplace and the business world.*

For solopreneurs:

- *People are your clients, your competitors, your peers, and others who work in your industry. They could also be the professional connections who you reach out to as part of your broader networking — for example, 'women in business' groups and other business groups.*

- *Identifying the people who you want to work with is crucial to establishing and refining your position on the market — including your USP, your services or products, and even your marketing strategies.*

- *Your personal brand is a major part of your USP and is what separates you from other solopreneurs offering similar services and solutions. Use your personal brand to connect with the people at the heart of your client relationships and connections.*

Stage 4:
Proposition

"If people like you, they will
listen to you - but if they trust
you, they'll do business
with you."

- Zig Ziglar

In the second chapter of this book, we identified the experiences, skills, and expertise which form the foundations of your personal brand story. We then moved on to the customers you're appealing to and how best to define your target customer for more direct and efficient marketing.

Now it's time to combine all of this as we move on to discuss brand authority – that is, what makes you, your business, and your overarching company a reputable and trustworthy place to do business?

In order to distinguish how best to promote your personal brand, you first need to know and understand exactly what it is you are promoting – in essence, what is your 'proposition'. Only when you have established your core offer, your value, and the right audience, can you plan and implement the right marketing activity to drive conversion.

Your personal brand proposition model:

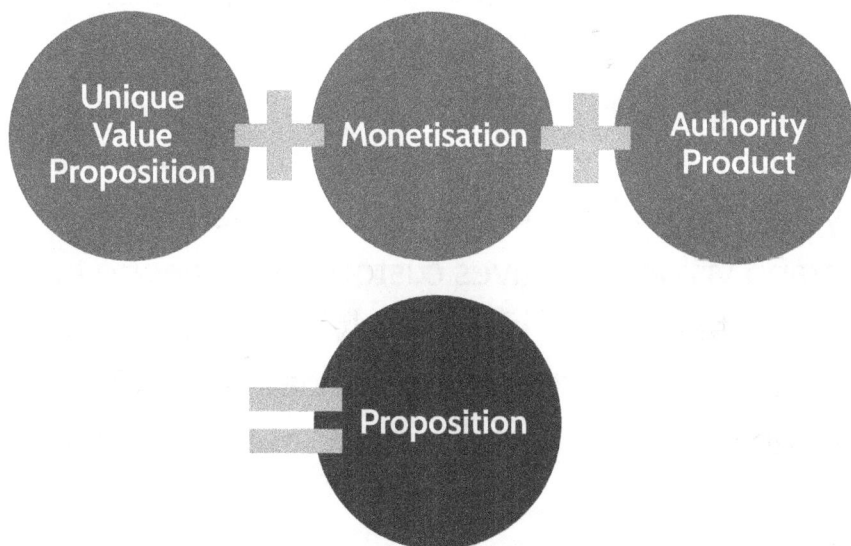

Unique Value Proposition **+** Monetisation **+** Authority Product

= Proposition

And it starts with your unique value proposition...

1. Unique Value Proposition (UVP)

A Unique Value Proposition (UVP) gives you a chance to tell the audience how you can help them, influence them, and provide a solution to their pain point or challenge. *The emphasis here is on you – and what makes you, as a business or solopreneur, the best suited to them as a client or customer.

Of course, it's not all on you as an individual. This aspect of your personal brand looks at you both as an individual and as a figure within a wider brand or organisation. It communicates to your target audience why they should choose to work with you and contract your services, and what makes you different from your competition – whether you work alone, under the umbrella of a brand or business you own, or as part of a larger organisation.

Your unique value proposition is what enables you to cut through the noise of the business world and stand out from the competition. It empowers you to attract the clients who are the best fit for your services, by combining your personal brand with your business or brand vision. This gives customers someone to resonate with and buy directly from, while still ensuring that level of professionalism which establishes trust and reputation in the product or service itself.

AND remember –

You are NOT selling products...

You are NOT selling services...

You ARE selling solutions!

Consider:

- *What sets you apart from others in your field — either in your business or across competitor organisations?*

- *Do you have a unique skillset or a particular area of expertise as a solopreneur?*

- *Does your business have a brand story or experience that gives you a unique perspective?*

Once you've answered these questions, you need to build a UVP which is integrated into everything you share online — from marketing collateral to professional profile updates and more.

A great place to start is to craft a compelling headline that describes the benefits you deliver — but keep it clear, succinct and free from meaningless, fluffy buzzwords.

As a **solopreneur**, this is the first touchpoint that introduces potential clients to what you do and how you can help them. It is your way of capturing exactly what value you offer, the problems you solve, and solutions you deliver.

As an **entrepreneur**, this is your personal portal to the business world you operate in – and solidifies the profile on which your business is built. Customers will look to you as the founder of the business, and want to see the UVP that you offer, which makes you and therefore your business reliable and trustworthy.

As an **intrapreneur**, this is what connects you as a professional to the role you do and the industry you work in. It grounds your position in expertise which is, in turn, good for the business you work for. Your UVP should herald the value you bring to your company, and the value your company delivers to customers.

Create your Unique Value Proposition (UVP) using the following formula:

Hello, I'm *(your personal brand name)*

A *(what you are / do — think solutions rather than titles)*

Helping *(target audience — be specific — think niche)*

Achieve *(value proposition)*

Whatever your UVP is, make sure it forms part of your marketing collateral and customer conversations alike.

2. Monetising your proposition

Having coached, trained and mentored many solopreneurs and small business owners, this is by far one of the most difficult and complex decisions to make — how much should I charge for my work?

And there are always two fundamental trains of thought that come with this:

- If I charge too much, I may price myself out of the marketplace — being perceived as expensive, unreasonable, or unaffordable, which can lead to a lack of interest in my offerings and potentially a negative impression of my brand!

However...

- If I charge too little, I may initially attract customers – but be perceived as too cheap, low value and low quality. Ultimately, I could undervalue my skills, experience, and expertise!

As a solopreneur, monetising your skills and expertise is essential to the success of your business. However, it can be challenging to set prices and payment rates for your time and work, especially when you're just starting.

And it's not just solopreneurs who struggle with this – with salary assuming a similar role in the professional life of an intrapreneur, and entrepreneurs facing similar challenges with regards to pricing their products and assigning their position in the market. Do you make your products and services more widely accessible while running the risk of undervaluing your skills, expertise, and quality? Or do you position yourself at the top of the market and run the risk of being regarded as too expensive?

Here are some actionable points to help you consider how to monetise your skills and expertise confidently – placing yourself, your products, and your skills on the right level of the market:

- **Identify your value proposition:** I've mentioned this already (see above) but determining what sets you apart from the competition and what value you can offer to your audience is essential. How unique are you / your products / your services?

- **Research the market:** Conduct market research to understand what your competitors charge for similar services or products. This will give you an idea of what the market can bear and will help you price competitively.

- **Determine your pricing strategy:** Decide on a pricing strategy that aligns with your goals and the value you offer. Consider factors such as the complexity of the project, the amount of time required, and your experience and expertise.

- **Offer different pricing options:** Provide your audience with different pricing options to choose from, such as a one-time fee, a retainer, or a subscription. This will increase the flexibility of your business model and cater to different budgets.

- **Communicate your value:** Communicate the value you offer to your audience through your marketing materials and communication channels. This will help your audience understand why your pricing is justified.

- **Continuously assess your pricing:** Continuously assess your pricing strategy and adjust it as needed to reflect changes in the market and your business.

Setting prices and payment rates can be a challenging task for any solopreneur or entrepreneur and can also play a part in salary negotiations for intrapreneurs as professionals continue to recognise their value and request salaries that reflect it.

Whatever bracket you fall into, it's important to remember that the decisions you make now are not forever, and that every company regardless of size and industry revisits pricing on a regular basis to remain competitive but profitable. So, if you don't get it right first time, learn from it and make changes.

Finally, one piece of advice that I've certainly learnt the hard way: don't allow your pricing to be dictated solely by the end product or service that you are selling. Remember that the background expertise and skillset you bring to the table is just as valuable as the end product, as it is what facilitates such a high-quality product in the first place.

For example, if you are a solopreneur running your own copywriting business, each article you written is not merely a standalone piece of unique content but also a culmination of the years of experience and skills building as you developed and honed that talent for content writing. Undercharging only serves to lessen the value of the years of time and experience that you have channelled into your business.

3. Authority Product

Building authority around your personal brand is essential for establishing credibility and growing your business. Whether you are a freelancer, a consultant, an employee, or an entrepreneur, your authority is what sets you apart from the competition and earns the trust of potential clients or customers – both for you personally and for the brand name under which you operate.

When you demonstrate your knowledge and expertise in your field, potential clients or customers are more likely to trust you and choose to work with you.

In order to achieve this and deliver it in a truly cohesive way, I would strongly recommend that you create an 'authority product' – a piece of work which will not only position your personal brand authority and expertise in your chosen industry or sector, but also generate numerous other revenue opportunities. These include but are not limited to **public speaking and TED Talks; guest interviews and public appearances; training workshops; guest lectures and seminars – essentially anything which puts your expertise and experience under the spotlight.**

There are three types of authority product which have proved extremely successful for many solopreneurs and entrepreneurs alike:

Write a book, research report or whitepaper

Writing a book, research report or whitepaper can be a highly effective way to establish your authority and grow your business – it has definitely worked for me!

By sharing your knowledge and expertise in a formal publication, you can demonstrate your credibility and position yourself as a thought leader in your field.

However, the process of planning, writing and publishing your work can be overwhelming.

Here are some actionable tips to help you get started...

- **Choose a topic that aligns with your expertise and interests:**

  The first step in planning a book, research report or whitepaper is to choose a topic that aligns with your expertise and interests. Consider the challenges and questions that your target audience faces and how you can address them through your writing.

  Create an outline that includes the key topics you want to cover and the main points you want to make. This will help you organise your thoughts and ensure that your work is cohesive and focused.

- **Research your subject:**

  Before you start writing, it's important to research your subject such as theories, models or industry case studies and statistics. This will help you tailor your writing to their specific interests and ensure that your book, research report or whitepaper is relevant and valuable to them.

  Conduct surveys or interviews with your target audience to gather insights and feedback. Use this information to inform your writing and ensure that your work resonates with your audience.

- **Develop a writing schedule:**

  Writing a book, research report or whitepaper takes time and discipline, so it's important to develop a writing schedule that works for you. Set aside dedicated time each day or week, and hold yourself accountable to this schedule.

Break down your writing schedule into smaller, manageable tasks or 'chunks'. This could include writing a certain number of pages each day or week, or completing specific sections of your outline.

- **Get feedback from beta readers:**

  Once you've completed a draft of your book, research report or whitepaper, it's important to get feedback from beta readers. These are individuals who can provide constructive criticism and feedback to help you improve your writing and refine your message.

  Reach out to friends, colleagues, or other professionals in your field and ask them to review your work. Provide them with a set of questions or prompts to guide their feedback.

- **Edit and revise:**

  After you've received feedback from beta readers, it's time to edit and revise your work. This process involves refining your writing, improving the structure and flow, and ensuring that your message is clear and concise.

  Create a checklist of editing and revision tasks to ensure that you address all the feedback you've received. This could include improving your writing style, eliminating redundancies, and tightening your message.

- **Consider self-publishing:**

  Finally, consider self-publishing your book, research report or whitepaper on platforms like Amazon or selling it directly through your website or specialist industry websites.

  There are plenty of commercial opportunities to sell your work, so you will need to research the self-publishing process and choose a distribution channel that aligns with your goals and budget.

Develop a signature course or membership

Planning and launching a signature course or membership can be an excellent way to leverage your expertise and generate income.

A signature course or membership can provide you with a flexible schedule and location independence, allowing you to work from anywhere in the world and design your workday according to your needs and preferences.

It also provides a scalable business model that can provide passive income streams and reduce the need for constant marketing and sales efforts. Once you've created your course or membership, it can be sold to an unlimited number of customers, allowing you to increase your revenue without having to invest significant time and effort.

However, the process can be overwhelming without a solid plan and strategy.

Here are some actionable points to help you plan and launch your signature course or membership:

- **Define your niche:** Identify your area of expertise and target audience to create a course that meets their needs and provides value.

- **Research:** Conduct market research to understand your competition and identify gaps in the market that you can fill with your course.

- **Develop your curriculum:** Create a curriculum (the planned sequence of educational and learning information) that aligns with your target audience's needs, is engaging, and provides actionable insights.

- **Choose your delivery method:** Decide on the delivery method for your course or membership, such as online video modules, live webinars, or in-person such as group workshops.

- **Launch strategy:** Develop a launch strategy that includes pre-launch marketing, email campaigns, social media promotions, and targeted advertising. This is often one of the most overlooked areas, so make sure you set time aside to plan and execute your launch strategy.

- **Pricing:** Determine the pricing for your course or membership that is competitive and offers value to your audience.

For a membership, you may choose to drip feed content using a monthly subscription-based model. Alternatively, you may provide all the content up front with a flexible monthly payment plan, as part of an agreed 12-month commitment.

- **Feedback:** Collect feedback from your audience and use it to improve your course or membership continually.

Create a coaching or mentoring program

Creating your own coaching or mentoring program can be rewarding both professionally and personally. It will enable you to share your experience, knowledge and skills to motivate others into changing or even transforming their business or lives. You may even consider it to be the next step after writing and publishing your book, research report or whitepaper.

Whether you choose to provide private 1-1 or group sessions (or even a mix of both), coaching and mentoring programs are highly scalable and flexible in delivery – as long as you have a laptop or mobile device and internet connection, you can pretty much coach and mentor anywhere in the world!

Furthermore, a signature course or coaching program can help you establish yourself as an authority in your field, which can lead to additional opportunities, such as speaking engagements, media interviews, and consulting projects. By developing a strong reputation and following, you can expand your reach and grow your business.

Here are some actionable points to help you plan and launch your coaching program:

- **Be clear about your expertise:** You are primarily helping and guiding people to maximise their own performance and enhance their productivity in a particular area or specialism, and this requires experience, knowledge and in some cases, industry-specific qualifications and accreditations.

- **Develop your coaching program curriculum:** Create a coaching program curriculum that aligns with your target audience's needs, is engaging, and provides actionable insights.

- **Choose your coaching delivery method:** Decide on the delivery method for your coaching program, such as one-on-one coaching, group coaching, or online coaching – or even a mix of all three!

- **Determine your pricing strategy:** Decide on a pricing strategy that aligns with your goals and the value you offer. Consider factors such as the complexity of the coaching program, the amount of time required, and your experience and expertise.

- **Establish yourself as an authority:** Establish yourself as an authority in your field through thought leadership, publishing articles and blog posts, and speaking at events.

- **Collect feedback:** Collect feedback from your clients and use it to improve your coaching program continually.

Authority product inspiration for intrapreneurs

For intrapreneurs, the concept of an authority product is different – largely because everything you do is managed and operated under the umbrella of the company you work for, and so any piece of content you produce publicly is shared under the company name.

However, that doesn't mean there are not still opportunities for you to establish your personal brand authority through valuable content – demonstrating your business prowess and skillset to both colleagues and customers alike.

Some of the following ideas are well suited to those in an intrapreneurship position, and range from large projects to smaller and more everyday interactions and communications which help to build trust:

- A training or mentoring program to help, guide and support colleagues or new employees
- A research paper or long form piece of content developed for or on behalf of the business
- Email updates for clients and customers, on the products or services that you think they might like
- Communication and check in with long term customers, demonstrating professional relationship nurturing

Don't forget to validate your authority product

Before launching any authority product, it's essential to gauge genuine demand. Validating your idea will ensure there's a target audience who are willing and potential ready to buy. It will also help in refining your idea and understanding your audience better. Validation can be achieved through a series of steps:

- **Online communities:** Engage in related groups to gauge what knowledge or support people are seeking.
- **Landing Page:** Set up a page for your product and see if people sign up.
- **MVP (Minimum Viable Product):** Release a pared-down version of your product. Gather feedback, learn from it, and then refine your offering.
- **Trial offerings:** For a book, course or membership, consider a pilot launch or preview content. For coaching, offer introductory sessions.

Make it work for you...

For solopreneurs:

Your proposition is what encourages clients to choose you over the next freelancer they come across. It combines your personality and ability to communicate with your skillset and experience, the way you portray your USP and UVP, and the way you deliver value through your authority product.

For entrepreneurs:

While your personal brand remains important when it comes to establishing and building brand authority, the main proposition that your customers are concerned with is that which is being offered by your business directly. They want to see good value and high quality in every product or service they buy or engage with and will be looking for the signs of a solid reputation in order to become long term and committed customers.

For intrapreneurs:

Your proposition gives you an edge as a professional and benefits your business by aligning you directly with customers and clients. Building your personal brand authority and establishing your skillset and expertise in the industry you work in is good for business, with companies needing to utilise committed intrapreneurs to greater effect if they want to really connect with the modern audience who buy from people rather than brand logos.

Stage 5:
Promotion

This is the part where you start considering how your personal brand should impact and inform your marketing activity – both online and offline. The multitude of touchpoints now available to professionals means that, for many of us, it feels like we always have to be "switched on" – that is, thinking about what we are saying and sharing, and how the messages we put out there could be connected back to our brand and professional profile.

In this chapter of the book, I'm going to share how to use the different marketing and connective touchpoints to harness a positive personal brand, without trapping you in a loop of 24/7 non-stop business talk.

Whether you're an entrepreneur, solopreneur, or intrapreneur, it can be easy to feel like every profile you manage online should be tailored towards your end customer – after all, you never who might find you or where. But this must always be tinted with balance, which is why you'll notice so many successful entrepreneurs in particular use their professional profiles as a bridge between their personal lives and business lives.

When you share personal motivations alongside business goals, tell followers and connections about upcoming trips and experiences that as personal as they are professional, and even announce personal milestones and goals, you create a rich online community of people who support **you** for **you**. They become people who acknowledge your personal life as they admire your professional expertise, and who use those more personal updates and shares as part of the reason why you stand out from competitors.

In short, it injects a more human side to your interactions – making you the kind of likable employee, solopreneur, or entrepreneur that makes people want to buy from and connect with you (and in turn, your brand or business). Thus, personal brand promotion should enable us to get much closer and grow a more meaningful relationship with our community.

What better way to do this than with content which connects our existing audience with our target audience – clients, suppliers, colleagues, and other stakeholders.

Your personal brand promotion model:

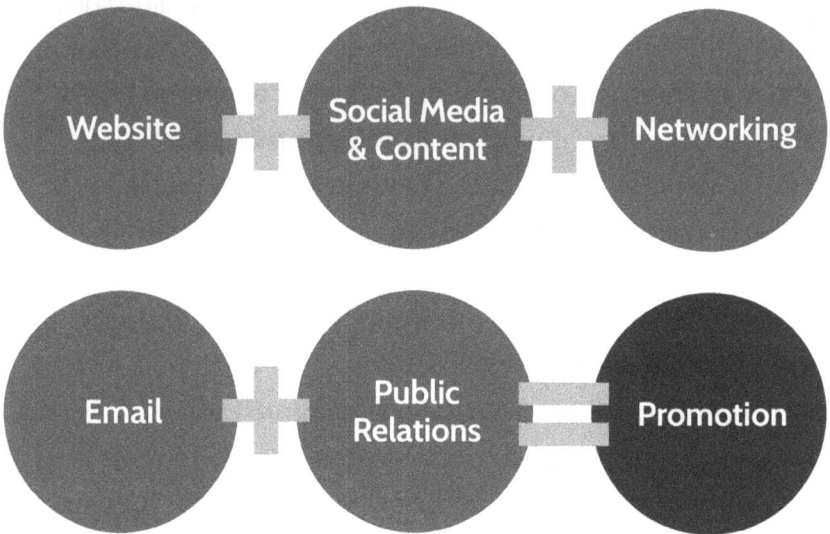

Website **+** Social Media & Content **+** Networking

Email **+** Public Relations **=** Promotion

Personal brand ecosystem

Engage, nurture, grow, repeat...

Your 'Personal Brand Ecosystem' aims to provide direction when it comes to communicating, promoting and delivering your personal brand experience to your target audience. For a business owner or entrepreneur, this means finding ways of talking to your existing audience, integrating value into the nurture process and using insight to encourage your audience to share, engage, and help you to expand your circle even wider.

Crucially, it draws together the tangible and intangible elements of your personal brand wheel, focusing on the most effective tools and channels across digital and traditional marketing environments. Of course, regardless of where you sit in the professional sphere, the most effective channels and platforms for you and for your audience will be different - which is where an understanding of your Circle of Influence comes into play – namely your target customers.

Find out where the customers you most want to connect with hang out online, what types of content they consume, how they are commonly introduced to and engage with their favourite brands, and what you can do to stand out to them.

Let's now delve in deeper to the essential tools you may choose to promote your personal brand – with a specific focus on the customers within your target audience. While personal brand promotion covers all corners of your target audience including colleagues and professional connections and peers, for the purpose of this book and helping you to define your best self for customers, we're sharing all the different marketing and promotional tools and how to harness their power for customer outreach.

1. Your website

There are currently over 1.8 billion active websites – and growing!

Your website is your virtual marketing and sales hub, introducing both active and prospective customers to your brand, your products, and your business as a whole. It is one of the most essential (and 100% controllable) tools in your brand promotion toolkit – your 24/7 365-day virtual marketing, sales and brand positioning hub!

Ultimately, any form of marketing when promoting your personal brand, whether social media, PR, print or events - should lead directly to your website as an information, education, brand positioning and sales 'hub' – capturing those valuable enquiries and sales leads. Consider your homepage your virtual shop window – giving users a direct look at what you're offering and enticing them inside. As such, it and all the pages beyond need to be representative of your brand and your offering, but concise and easy to unpick; comprehensive in information, as well as aesthetically pleasing and easy to use.

Plan a user-friendly navigation structure

The success of any website is based on clear and intuitive navigation. Websites are no longer just a virtual environment to talk about yourself; rather, we must consider and plan the desired 'journey' you would like each user to take across your site.

Implement the three-click principle, whereby visitors to the website must be able to find the information they require within three clicks of the mouse – no matter what their starting point.

This requires a detailed site map which finds links between all the different pages via CTA and other action buttons, menus, and embedded links.

Design a homepage that creates desire and generates intent

The main objectives of a high performing homepage are two-fold: to re-enforce the brand and its positioning within the marketplace; and to present an aggregation of the website's current / most-relevant content in order to appeal to the user during those crucial first five seconds of a new user's visit.

To make this achievable, consider applying:

- o Header / banner image at the top of the page, with strong, engaging brand image and your positioning statement;
- o A welcome message leading into a strong positioning statement, representing core services complemented by key messages;
- o Clear call-to-actions such as 'find out more' or 'contact me' using colourful buttons, icons and promotion pods directing visitors to specific sections of the site;
- o Strong visual / emotive imagery which draws interest and ignites a desire to learn more;
- o A selection of testimonials which reinforces brand positioning and quality of service;
- o Links to your Blog posts;
- o Ultimately – keep it simple, jargon free and user friendly visually and emotively!

The underlying incentive of your website will of course depend on your business model and industry.

Entrepreneurs are most likely to use the homepage to introduce the brand itself.

Solopreneurs will place more emphasis on their personal brand and direct experience / expertise. Take care to define what matters most to the user – i.e., do they immediately want to know who you are and what you can offer to them, or are they more interested in the products and solutions you can deliver?

If you're an **intrapreneur,** this same guidance can be used to inspire and inform changes to your professional profile – creating a headline bio which connects to some of your professional achievements in a more concise way.

Provide meaningful 'human-focused' information

It still surprises me how many businesses make the fatal mistake of being non-human when it comes to presenting their brand across their website.

Don't get me wrong - being corporate is fine. Being formal is fine. However, building a website on rigid corporate messages, scripted sales promos and jargon, not.

Businesses that choose to communicate in this way are the opposite of engaging – and as a result they push website visitors away.

To grow mutually beneficial relationships, entice users to convert into paying customers, and to encourage customer loyalty, we must make an effort to 'humanise' how we communicate and present our brand across our website and beyond.

Each piece of information (text, videos, images, etc.) needs to have a reason to exist. The easiest way to determine the value of every content section on your website is to look at it from your customer's point of view – is it useful, friendly, educational and engaging?

Focus on providing real and authentic value rather than simply building keywords and vainly trying to improve SEO.

And finally, mix it up!

Consider a range of content styles which each enable you to present information on your website. From regular blog posts and videos to podcasts, infographics, and free downloadable eBooks.

Link to your social media

Social media is the most powerful (and free) tool for building a community of followers and fans. What's more, with so many social platforms available, there truly is a network for every business, solopreneur, industry, and user – with different demographics in touch via different platforms and social channels.

In order to nurture a connected and cohesive online presence, it is essential to link your website to your Facebook, Twitter, LinkedIn or Instagram account and vice versa.

Have social media sharing buttons on your main service pages and, just as importantly, on your blog posts, as these allow people to quickly share what you are saying with their friends, collegues and followers - thus increasing engagement!

Make it mobile

Whether you run your own business, work for someone else's business, or manage a solopreneur presence, you will almost certainly be familiar with the concept of a responsive website – that is, a website that responds to different screen sizes and configurations, and adjusts the layout accordingly.

Mobile has become the dominant platform on which people choose to view a website, meaning it is essential that your website is 'responsive' and able to be used across all manner of different platforms.

In addition, it is also becoming increasingly popular for homepages to be longer, and more "scrollable" – giving users access to more information on a single page, rather than forcing them to navigate around your site via a multitude of buttons and menu options (which are, let's be honest, difficult to use on a mobile device).

Your website may not be the first place that a user or prospective customer finds you and your brand or business, but if they are interested in what you are offering then it is likely the place where they will end up. What that means is that your website needs to support the user experience regardless of where they come from and what stage of the conversion funnel they are at when they arrive.

The above advice covers a range of focus points for an efficient website – however, this is just a starting point. As a business owner, solopreneur, or intrapreneur, it is up to you to determine what your customers or audience want to know and how to share that information with them – embracing the brand story we created earlier in this book and using that, your personal brand, and what you know about your customers to create a concise and cohesive online journey for them.

With that said, it's time we tackled the giant of the digital marketing world, and the trend which is certainly not budging anytime soon – whether we like it or not.

Yes, it's social media time.

2. Social media

Social media is an invaluable communication tool for any business especially when it comes to engaging with our ideal audience, growing a community of loyal followers and fans, and creating brand authority online. But how do we harness that power for the benefit of our personal brand, and how should entrepreneurs, solopreneurs, and intrapreneurs all use social media?

For **solopreneurs**, social media is a way of building that brand authority we talk so much about, while connecting your service and business persona with your presence as a skilled individual. It's a way of connecting and building engagement with clients, while also highlighting your skills and sharing value with followers to nurture prospective future connections and relationships.

For **entrepreneurs**, social media is a marketing tool which connects your most captive audience with your products and the solutions that you provide. It enables users, customers, prospective customers to explore your products, learn more about your brand, and access existing user reviews and testimonials – while also getting an idea as to the personal brand which shrouds the business brand in authority and reliability. Not only that, but social media enables brands to build communities – connecting likeminded users and delivering value every day through content shares and more.

For **intrapreneurs**, social media can become the platform which connects you with your industry outside of the role you hold in a company or business. A finessed and finetuned social media account can allow you to become somewhat of an influential figure in your industry outside of your job role – giving you a platform through which to share your experiences and link to your role but through your own voice. Out of all the tools available in your armoury, social media is the platform that gives intrapreneurs the most freedom and flexibility with regards to content – provided you harness and use it correctly.

Social media should, in essence, define and support the values of your business with clarity; instil confidence and trust in connections and customers through your own knowledge; and form an effective and memorable way of communicating with your audience.

It is an inherently sociable marketing tool, which is as effective (if not more so) when approached as an engagement and direct communication platform, as it is when used for marketing.

While social media does support paid ads and advertising blocks, for the most part it is a way for brands across all industries to grow a following and find ways of reaching out to, engaging with, and enticing their ideal audience into following them - thus becoming part of their brand community.

Here are some tips to help you put your personal brand front and centre on every social platform.

Make sure your profile is professional

We begin with one of the most essential elements to promote the visual aspect of your personal brand on social media – your personal profile.

They say a picture is worth a thousand words and never has this been truer than when selecting the main profile photo. When selecting your image, consider the perspective of future and prospective customers, clients, and employers. Does your image evoke trust, and present a friendly individual that they might want to do business with?

When outlining your role or position in a profile bio, go beyond your bog-standard job title. Again, consider who your target audience is and what you truly offer, focusing on the solutions you provide and facilitate through your work.

For example:

> If you were a **solopreneur**, you might say something like "I help clients to double their monthly sales through exquisite copy".

> If you were an **entrepreneur**, your role will connect to the position you play within your company or business – as founder, managing director, or something more creatively linked to the business, brand, or industry. (I've seen lots of variations on the CEO concept in my time, including 'Chief Happiness Officers' and more!)

> If you were an **intrapreneur** working for an events decorating company, you might consider something creative like "Beautifying the events world one venue at a time".

Putting solutions in the direct eyeline of prospective and potential customers is key to establishing quick authenticity and trust.

And finally, don't neglect your banner image at the top of your profile (where applicable). Your profile acts as your very own corner of 'Internet real estate' – and it's free! Use this space to present what you do in a visual context, with imagery which is directly connected to a service you provide, or with product imagery from your business.

Keep your content light and easy to consume

Social media is a place where people go to scroll, usually filling their leisure time while occasionally learning – and almost always on the hunt for entertaining and relatable content. Posting big blocks of marketing copy or a breakdown of your day isn't going to entice or inspire anyone. Nor are hard hitting sales pitches or aggressive marketing campaigns which try too hard to sell.

Share quotes, snippets of insight into your day or your business, and break down the barriers which exist between your brand and your customers – creating the kind of connection which adds personality, and which makes your brand or business more relatable via the people behind the scenes.

In addition to the tone of the content, consider using a mix of media from image posts to short videos, infographics to gifs. All have their merit and will enhance engagement and interaction.

Provide backstage insight into your office environment or team

People buy from authentic people, and when they can see who you work with and where you work, they will start to picture themselves interacting with that team - rather than just your brand name or logo.

It helps to humanise your brand by presenting an authentic snapshot of life behind the scenes. This will also make your brand seem more trustworthy and reliable.

Social media is all about engagement, and that means responding to comments and messages that you receive!

You wouldn't believe how many users put a post out there and then ignore all the comments - undoing all of that hard work!

But as I've always said:
'It isn't social media if you aren't being social'

Your social media 'community' want to feel appreciated and respected, and you must use your platform to build personal brand authority by being personable. Encourage engagement at any opportunity and always thank people if they like, comment on, or share your content. When you respond, you encourage people to comment more, and will find that you build a rapport with your audience.

And yes, the same is true for negative comments and potentially controversial reactions. In fact, if anything, this is even more important than responding to the positive feedback and engagement because it demonstrates a commitment on your part to monitoring consumer response and adjusting your business or service provision to that response.

If customers highlight an issue with one of your products or share negative feedback about a service they received, use the public channel to express your apology and how you plan to improve moving forward. And if their negative views are unfounded and unfair, proceed with grace but confidence in your business.

You can't please everyone!

Create partnerships with likeminded businesses and business individuals, and share great stories from inside your industry.

It's not called 'social networking' for nothing!

A big part of building personal brand authority is showing that both you and your brand are at the forefront of the industry and have tons of knowledge, experience and value to share. As such, professional networking can be a very powerful asset when developing and growing your personal brand.

And, if you can identify the right people and nurture those relationships, you can develop a strong and lasting network, which could benefit you for years to come.

It has for me – and still does!

Be consistent

This one is so important, and contrary to popular believe it does not mean posting every day. Instead, being consistent means posting regularly enough that you start to become a reliable source of content on a regular and predictable basis.

Keep showing up - your followers need to see that you are present. Plan your content accordingly. Repetition is key, but always share content in a different and creative way.

And remember to keep focused on your brand positioning, brand image and tone of voice throughout. This facilitates that all-important multichannel success, regardless of whether you work alone, as part of an existing company, or building your own brand.

3. Content

Content is a huge part of building and nurturing your personal brand, primarily because it supports every single area that we have touched on so far.

Content has the power to connect you with customers or clients, to entice new followers into joining you, and to promote and express exactly who you are and what you are about – both as an individual and as part of a brand personality.

It can also provide you with an outlet to establish some of the core areas of focus, such as expertise and experience, and can build into a neat hierarchy of information that you share sporadically with your audience for ongoing engagement and development.

One of the biggest things you need to remember about content, regardless of the channel you're posting on, is the importance of VALUE.

Your target audience do not want to be sold to - rather, they are far more likely to respond to a conversation, a discussion, or an invitation that feels personal and direct to them. If every piece of content you share has an underlying sales message, you cannot expect to build that authentic and transparent personal brand. Instead, you will be viewed as a salesperson and nothing more.

This is especially challenging for intrapreneurs as finding the purpose behind your content can be a difficult element to bridge.

Do you create content on behalf of the company you work for, or do you use your platform to demonstrate your expertise and skill within the industry you work for but on a more independent basis?

The answer to this will depend on your motivation and what you want to achieve, though I would always say that getting your expertise front and centre benefits both you and the business you work for when done well.

Whatever your motivation and content output, the truest success comes from a connection with those customers who see you as the solution they're looking for.

From blogs, GIFs, memes, and infographics, through to templates and checklists the plethora of content choices is endless and really depends on your target audience. However, there are currently two types of content which are considered among the most accessible and which have made waves in the modern marketing sector: videos and podcasts. Let's have a look at these in more detail.

Videos

Video has rapidly become an essential tool for building and promoting your personal brand. With the rise of social media and digital platforms, creating video content has never been easier – and its benefits are unrivalled.

By creating video content that showcases your personality, expertise, and unique perspective, you can connect with your audience in a way that is both engaging and authentic; not to mention it underpins that important idea of people buying from people, by giving them a direct line of sight into the individuals and experts behind the business name and brand logo.

Here are some reasons why you may want to consider adding video to your personal brand promotion mix:

- **Video allows you to showcase your unique personality and perspective in a way that written content simply can't. It's an excellent tool for solopreneurs seeking new clients, entrepreneurs looking to make their mark in a jampacked industry, and even intrapreneurs who want to ground their employer and themselves in industry expertise.**

By creating engaging video content that speaks to your audience, you can connect with them on a deeper level and establish a sense of authenticity and trust.

- **Video content has the potential to go viral and reach a wider audience than written content alone.**

With the right combination of engaging content, promotion, and audience targeting, your videos have the potential to become a powerful tool for brand awareness and growth.

- **Video can help you establish yourself as a thought leader in your industry.**

By consistently creating valuable video content that speaks to your audience's needs and interests, you can position yourself, your brand, or even your employer as an expert and a go-to resource in your field.

- **Brand Videos** - Brand videos are primarily for raising awareness of your products and services. They're particularly helpful for start-ups who are, as yet, unknown in the marketplace.

- **Explainer Videos** - Do you need to explain something about your products or business? If so, snappy, intuitive explainer videos can help. They offer your target audience a quickfire way of getting to grips with what you do, without having to wade through dull written guides and instructions.

- **Event Videos** - Event videos are a great addition for companies at conferences and shows. They let you put your best foot forward and communicate loads of information quickly. This may include behind the scenes footage.

- **Live Videos** - Live video provides a 'live' snapshot into 'what's happening now' and has become hugely popular with many solopreneurs and entrepreneurs, especially as the major social media platforms such as Facebook, Instagram, TikTok, Twitter, and LinkedIn heavily cater to and promote this format.

- **Demonstration Videos** - Demonstration videos show your customers how they can benefit from using your products or services. This format is great when your customers are not sure why they should buy from you.

- **Interview and Podcast Videos** - Marketing and education are blending into one. Interview videos provide your audience with valuable content while securing brand authority. More about podcasts below!

There are many other video formats too: animated videos, videos that use augmented reality, and those that attempt to deliver personalised messages. The best ones for you to explore really depend on what you hope to achieve.

But regardless of your industry or area of expertise, investing in video content can help you connect with your audience, build brand awareness, and establish yourself as a thought leader with your target audience.

Podcasts

Podcasts have become increasingly popular in recent years due to advancement in mobile technology. Not only do they allow you to establish yourself as a thought leader in your industry, but they also offer a unique opportunity to connect with your audience on a personal level – using a format which is easy for users to access and enjoy on-the-go and at their leisure. By creating high-quality content that resonates with your listeners, you can build a loyal following and ultimately drive business growth.

One of the key benefits of podcasts is their ability to offer a deep dive into a particular topic or issue. Whether you're discussing industry trends, sharing insights from experts in your field, or exploring new ideas and perspectives, podcasts allow you to connect with your audience in a way that is both informative and engaging.

In addition, podcasts provide a platform for personal connection and relationship-building. By sharing your thoughts, experiences, and perspectives, you can create a sense of intimacy with your listeners that is difficult to achieve through other mediums.

This can help you build trust and credibility with your audience, which in turn can lead to increased engagement and conversions.

Before I share more on how to get started with podcasts in particular, I wanted to draw on one very clear trend which is making waves across the podcast and content sector – and it's one for all your intrapreneurs out there.

We are seeing more and more videos, podcasts, and even short form social media reels being released which focus on sharing the experiences of select professionals within an industry – sort of like a "beginners guide" style to certain topics, job roles, and professions. Creating an entire online platform based on "an insider's views on X" – breaking myths and giving insight into your industry – intrapreneurs can become influencers in their own right.

You only have to look at the number of wedding planners from venues around the world sharing wedding planning tips, or flight attendants sharing funny stories, or animal shelter employees sharing the cutest animals onsite, to see how this kind of accessible content creates a platform on which to highlight the industry and role you work in.

Here are four actionable points to help you get started with a podcast:

- **Identify your niche**
  The first step in creating a successful podcast is identifying your niche.

  What topics are you passionate about?
  What unique perspective can you offer?

  By narrowing down your focus and offering something truly valuable to your audience, you'll be more likely to attract loyal listeners and establish yourself as a thought leader in your industry.

- **Create high-quality content**

  Once you've identified your niche, it's time to start creating high-quality content that resonates with your audience. This could include interviews with experts in your field, solo episodes where you share your thoughts and insights, or even live events or panel discussions.

  Whatever format you choose, make sure your content is engaging, informative, and consistent.

- **Promote your podcast**

  Don't forget to promote your podcast to get it in front of as many listeners as possible. This could include leveraging your social media channels, reaching out to other podcasters or influencers in your space, and even investing in paid advertising.

  The key is to make sure you're targeting the right audience and providing them with a compelling reason to tune in.

- **Be a guest on someone else's podcast**

  When you guest star on a podcast, you get the added advantage of being endorsed by the podcast host as an expert. Moreover, engaging in lively interactions with the host can help you establish a stronger connection with listeners and enhance your reputation – and you might even pick up some ideas for engaging and chatting to your listeners.

Types of Podcast Promotion

- **Interview Podcasts** feature interviews with guests who share their experiences, knowledge, and expertise on a specific topic. The host often asks questions to gain insights and opinions from the guests, featuring one-to-one question and answer conversation, as well as more open dialogue.

- **News and Current Affairs Podcasts** focus on providing updates and analysis of current events, news, and political developments.

- **Educational and How-To Podcasts** provide information, instruction, and guidance on various topics, including self-improvement, career development, and personal finance.

- **Storytelling Podcasts** feature compelling stories, often with a narrative structure, that are intended to captivate and engage listeners.

- **Lifestyle Podcasts** focus on providing guidance and advice on various aspects of life, including health and wellness, relationships, and travel.

- **Specialist Interest Podcasts** - from sport and comedy, through to music and politics, these podcasts focus on providing commentary, analysis and entertainment for a wide and diverse audience.

Overall, podcasts offer a diverse range of content and can cater to a wide variety of interests and preferences. They are also a powerful tool for anyone looking to build and promote their personal brand – whether from the perspective of a solo venture, a new business, or a role within a larger company.

The 5E's model for creating content

Creating content which promotes your authority and expertise is a critical component of any successful personal brand. However, in today's fast-paced digital world, attention spans are short, and competition for audience engagement is fierce. Therefore, it's essential to create content that not only captures attention but also educates and ultimately converts viewers into customers.

Here's where my 5E's model will help and guide you through the thought process of creating content with value, which will work across all your promotion channels.

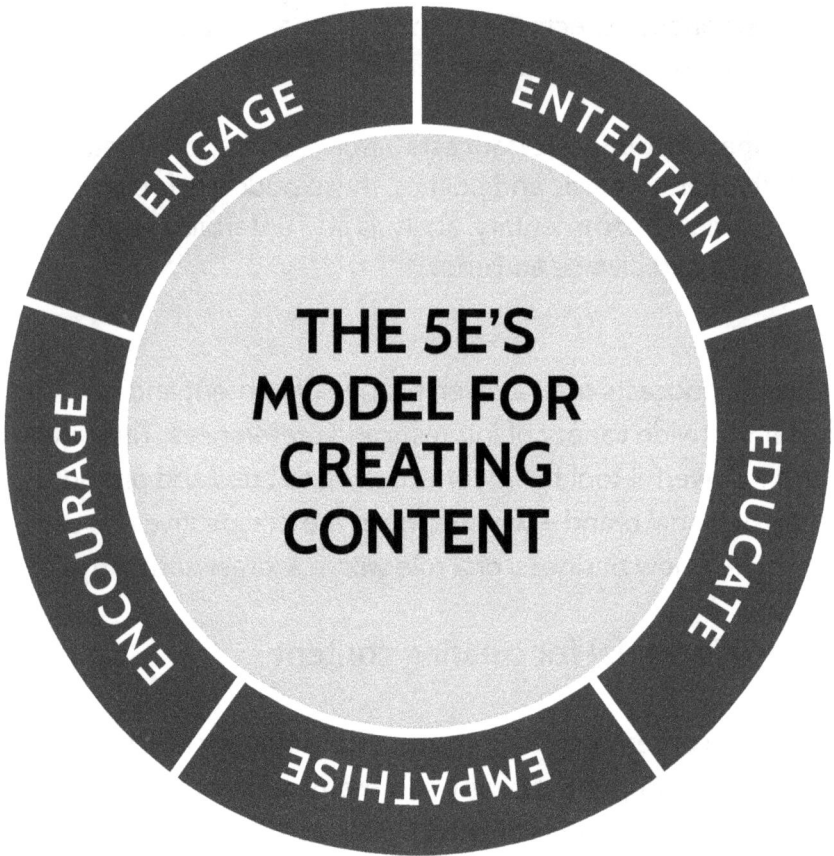

ENGAGE
ENTERTAIN
EDUCATE
EMPATHISE
ENCOURAGE

THE 5E'S MODEL FOR CREATING CONTENT

ENGAGE with your target audience by providing plenty of 'problem-solving' value such as top-tips, how-to guides, free trials and taster sessions.

Recommended Content:
Blogs, eBooks, image posts, quotes, memes and gifs, articles, quizzes, templates, checklists and challenges.

ENTERTAIN your target audience with your brand story, life experiences and inspirational anecdotes.

Recommended Content:
Video's, podcasts, virtual events, blogs and vlogs.

EDUCATE your target audience by showing them how your products / services could help solve their 'pain points' – and what differentiates you from your competitors. This is where we come back to that all important need to market yourself and brand / business as a solution rather than simply a supplier or seller.

Recommended Content:
Webinars, product demonstrations, infographics, long-form posts, Q&A's, case studies, eBooks and whitepapers.

EMPATHISE with your target audience - understand what challenges (or pain points) they are experiencing at this moment. How can you offer support or provide a solution?

Recommended Content:
Survey's, questionnaires, polls, interviews, action plans and private coaching groups.

ENCOURAGE regular dialogue with your target audience using your website, social media, email marketing and networking. Nurture your community and build mutually beneficial relationships!

Recommended Content:
User generated content, forum and private group discussions, email marketing, mastermind groups.

4. Networking

Many business professionals shy away from networking through fear and pressure of having to walk into a room full of strangers, start a conversation with someone they've never met before, and try to develop a relationship – all without coming across too 'salesy'.

However, as we have already established, 'people buy from (authentic) people' and there is no better opportunity than in a face-to-face environment.

Networking enables us to widen our physical reach, not just IN the room – but also THROUGH the room, via people we meet who can introduce us to others in their wider network.

Of course, not everyone goes in with the right attitude. I've heard some horror stories of senior managers sending their teams to various networking events, ordering them to return with handfuls of lucrative leads and then berating them for failing to do so!

What these types of individuals don't seem to understand is that networking is for the long game – not the quick win!

It is a two-way process for making connections and building mutually beneficial relationships.

Ultimately, proactive networking will enable you to:

- **AMPLIFY** your personal brand
- **REACH** the decision makers
- **WIDEN** your physical reach
- **BUILD TRUST** with your target audience
- **ENHANCE** your professional credibility - gaining referrals, testimonials and recommendations for your work
- **FIND** your next big career opportunity – new customer or job
- **SUSTAIN** your business connections and mutually beneficial relationships

This is true regardless of your professional position, with solopreneurs using networking to reach new clients and connect with peers who can help them to understand the complexity of the business world and adapt and grow accordingly; while intrapreneurs can use networking to further their career, and entrepreneurs can use it to ascertain where in the market they should position their brand or business.

How to use networking to your advantage

It all comes down to the way you present yourself and align yourself with others.

When your personal brand forms part of your overall business marketing strategy, aligning and connecting yourself with likeminded businesses and business owners immediately puts you in the same category as them.

Networking is about establishing and building connections, not only so that you can learn from those individuals but also so that your business becomes aligned and linked with them and their success.

There's a reason why businesses want to be seen at certain events, in the presence of certain business owners and entrepreneurs, and in attendance at certain award ceremonies - because it connects them to those individuals and their success rate. And that, in turn, allows their customer base and yours to become connected, interwoven, and one and the same.

Here are some tips for using networking to build your personal brand:

Be selective

There is a seemingly endless array of networking opportunities available both online and face-to-face. Trying to attend all of these events could be incredibly costly on your time, resources and more importantly, your hard-earned cash.

Experiment and attend different events at different levels within your industry, based on where you are now and where you want to be or what you want to achieve. This is especially true for intrapreneurs exploring different areas of business and opportunities, and solopreneurs who hope to grow and expand their influence.

Selecting the best events involves thinking outside of the box and inserting yourself into new, innovative, and often unexpected opportunities to create connections in different corners of the industry. This may include conferences, exhibitions, and trade shows. You never know when it might come in useful to know someone at a certain business or in a certain job role.

Do your research

Before you start your networking experience, consider your goals:

- Why are you attending this event?
- What do you actually want to achieve and with who?
- Is there a particular type of person you want to meet? If so, what do you hope to gain or learn from them?
- What level of seniority are they – what responsibilities do they hold? How easy are they going to be to reach and connect with?

- Are you attending an industry specific event (such as procurement, HR or marketing) or a more generic networking group where you will have access to a range of business owners and professionals from different sectors and interests?

Be prepared

Preparation is key if you want to gain the success from your networking opportunities.

Punctuality, smart appearance, and a generous handful of your own business cards have always been the staple requirement for serial networkers.

But that's not all.

In most cases you will be asked to 'present yourself'. This is essentially an opportunity to 'pitch' who you are and the product or services you offer. Crucially, this means sharing more than just your name, job title and waffle about your work

- Try and stay clear of job titles. Instead, consider your 'positioning statement' – how you solve your customer pain points; what differentiates you from your competitors.
- Share a story, anecdote or experience to support your positioning.
- Tell your audience who you have worked for and who you want to work with.
- Always finish with a referral request – someone you want to connect with or an organisation you would like an introduction too.

Building your 'online' network is just as important as your 'offline' environment

This became particularly important in terms of personal branding during the pandemic, with the most successful business owners and entrepreneurs being those who took to their social feeds and checked in with their networking groups regularly and consistently.

When you network with your peers and industry professionals in person, be sure to connect with them on LinkedIn and other professional platforms after the event or meeting. Make sure, when doing this, that you send a personalised connection request, rather than the default 'Billy Boring' invitation.

And remember... building your personal brand and forging valuable connections is a long game, and cultivating relationships takes time. The chances of the becoming an overnight client or a career progression opportunity after a single meeting are slim to none – but that doesn't mean the connection isn't worth pursuing, nurturing, and retaining in your armoury.

Show the real you in all your online content

The whole point of personal branding is to put yourself front and centre of your brand, and so displaying and showcasing the real you is what will ensure that the personal brand you put out to the world displays and celebrates the most relatable and trustworthy version of yourself.

Some things you can do include providing insight into behind-the-scenes footage from your office or workplace, sharing information on how you spend your free time, giving followers fun details or facts they might not know about you, and sharing more about your experiences and your brand story.

Networking is not just a small part of personal branding - it is, in essence, what will connect and link you to the most valuable, insightful, and personable contacts you can hope for in business.

Whether you are just starting out on your journey to build a personal brand or are already established and looking to expand your connections and customer net, networking is a way to meet new people, learn from them, and attract new audiences.

5. Recommendations / testimonials

Now it's time to sprinkle some gold dust over your personal brand promotion!

Word of mouth has long been the best and purest form of organic marketing, giving potential customers the peace of mind that your products can be trusted, that you are reliable to work with, and/or that your services are effective and offer good value.

For me as a solopreneur, word of mouth recommendations and testimonials are marketing gold dust – and they've frequently pitched me above far bigger businesses and corporations when it comes to securing client loyalty.

The reason why word of mouth is such a big deal when it comes to personal branding is that the power of someone's words hold far more weight than your own when it comes to compelling and reliable marketing.

Why?

Because consumers trust and relate to other consumers more than anyone else.

Word of mouth marketing helps build and promote your personal brand among your ambassadors, role models and influencers as well as customers and clients, garnering admiration and support among your entire audience.

The best time to ask for a recommendation or testimonial is immediately after finishing a specific project / job role / relationship. It would be advisable to approach senior representatives of the organisation who present some influence and responsibility – after all, who wouldn't trust a service recommended by the company CEO?

Start asking your trusted connections in your Circle of Influence for recommendations – whether they're customers, clients, suppliers, managers or trade partners – and build those glowing testimonials that back up all the marketing you do for your own personal brand.

6. Email marketing

Email marketing is a powerful tool for building and promoting your personal brand. It provides a direct line of communication with your audience and allows you to cultivate relationships with your subscribers.

By consistently delivering valuable content and personalised messaging, you can establish yourself as a thought leader in your industry and increase your influence – all while bolstering your soft sell marketing by consistently placing your brand name in the line of sight of captive customers and clients.

One of the key benefits of email marketing is its ability to reach a large audience quickly and easily. With the click of a button, you can send out a message to hundreds or thousands of subscribers, sharing important updates, news, and promotions. This can help you stay top-of-mind with your audience and ensure that they are always aware of what you are working on.

Here are five actionable points to help you get started:

Build your email list

The first step to successful email marketing is building a strong email list. There are a number of ways to do this, including:

- o Offering a lead magnet (like an e-book or a webinar) in exchange for email addresses

- o Promoting your blog and encouraging readership with inbound links to other valuable resources
- o Creating a subscription page on your website or setting up a dedicated landing page to capture email addresses
- o Including invites in your email signature and/or on your invoices
- o Approach existing contacts to subscribe to your email newsletter – and refer other people (word of mouth marketing in action again!)

It is important to remember that, since GDPR regulations were updated in 2020, you can only add someone to your list who has consented to do so. Once they have signed up, they must be given the option to opt out in every single email they receive.

List building is one of the most important stages in the process. However, it's all about quality over quantity – i.e., you need to obtain quality prospects, otherwise the information that you send out is not going to have the desired effect. Building a high-quality list takes time, patience and determination.

Use segmentation to personalise your messaging

You can't market to everyone – and why would you want to?

Take advantage of email marketing's powerful segmentation capabilities to personalise your messaging. There are literally hundreds of ways in which you can do this, but here are just a few:

- o Demographics
- o Business sector / industry
- o Interests
- o Geographical preferences
- o Previous products or services the customer has purchased from you
- o Promotions or special offers that the individual has participated in previously

By grouping subscribers based on their interests or behaviour, you can create targeted campaigns that speak directly to their needs and preferences. This not only increases engagement and conversions, but also helps to build stronger relationships with your subscribers over time.

Create valuable content

Email marketing is all about being strategic. Subscribers will quickly look for the unsubscribe button if they are constantly being bombarded with sales messages. The information that you send to your subscribers should be valuable to them.

Writing each email should be approached with care. After all, you only have a matter of seconds to capture the interest of the reader.

Create a benefit-focused, engaging title for your email accompanied by a suitable image. The main content in your email should be valuable to the reader, engaging and precise, followed by a few select links to related stories on your website, designed to increase click through rates.

Content should be varied including blog posts, articles which are exclusive to subscribers, and video content as well as news stories and occasional marketing offers which aim to generate a direct response.

You may also find that distributing announcements is a great way to engage with your audience, particularly if it relates to a product launch or a change in the business that would prove beneficial to customers.

Set and monitor your metrics

Email marketing is only effective if your strategies prove successful.

The only way that you can assess whether your campaigns are performing is to collect and evaluate key metrics. If you use a dedicated email marketing tool you can generate detailed reports within these applications.

Typical data that you can collect will include:

- o How many emails were opened
- o Number of emails which bounced back
- o The number of emails which were not opened
- o Click through statistics
- o The number of people who unsubscribed
- o Complaints about spam
- o Number of social shares

Use this data to fine tune your email marketing campaigns, focusing on strong areas and eliminating strategies which have proved less successful.

Consider utilising a third-party email marketing platform

Third-party email marketing platforms offer several benefits over trying to manage an email marketing campaign manually or through a basic email client.

Here are several reasons why:

- **Automation:** Schedule emails, set up action-triggered sequences, and personalise messages for different audience segments.

- **Scale:** Easily manage large volumes of emails and subscribers, a task that can be challenging with a basic email client.

- **Analyses:** Access detailed data on campaign performance such as open rates and conversions, to refine your strategy and improve outcomes.

- **Design:** Use pre-made templates and design tools to create professional-looking emails without needing advanced skills.

- **Deliverability:** Enjoy better email deliverability as these platforms strive to ensure your messages don't land in spam folders by maintaining good relationships with email providers.

- **Integration:** Sync your marketing efforts across channels by integrating with other digital tools like CRMs, e-commerce platforms, and social media.

Through targeted list building and effective planning, email marketing can prove to be a hugely beneficial marketing tool to building and promoting your personal brand.

While the benefits of this for **solopreneurs** and **entrepreneurs** are clear, enabling you to share updates from within your business and retain an open line of communication with customers and clients both active and dormant, for **intrapreneurs** email marketing is more likely something to take back to your role within the business. While this section is not necessarily conducive to your role, understanding the benefits of email marketing can help you to diagnose success points and potential issues with your company's marketing and help find solutions.

7. Public Relations

We have already talked about how important valuable content is when building up a captive audience, but if you don't shout about it then how will anybody find your great content?

Public Relations (or PR) is all about maintaining a favourable image with your target audience. PR is not just about corporate – it's also about personal brand too, and has as much to do with the way that colleagues, employers, clients, and customers feel about you personally as they do about your brand or company.

It's easy to think that PR is simply about getting your brand message out there, but it's a lot more nuanced than that. It's about using a wide range of tactics to build your brand. That could include:

- Going to local, national, and international events and networking with customers and other businesses directly.

- Building community connections through altruistic projects such as supporting local organisations, providing education, or making charitable donations.

Whether you are communicating in-house, to the general public, or other businesses, your personal brand needs to shine through. The messages need to be coherent, attractive and, above all, consistent across all channels.

When developing your strategy, you need to set goals, create key messages and choose the right tools and tactics, just as you would with any other marketing activity.

Use all your promotion outlets as a way of pushing your content out there, whether it's a blog, news article, opinion piece or a testimonial. Identify, research, nurture and grow...

Here are three actionable points to help you with your public relations:

- Identify the most appropriate (consumer or trade) platforms and networks across news and industry specific websites, authoritative blogs, forums and directories, newspaper and magazine publishers, television stations and radio channels.

- Research and follow specific #hashtags, keywords and search terms (Google Alerts) – for current editorial themes, trend-spotting, news-jacking, guest blogging opportunities, guest podcast and webinar interviews.

- Develop, nurture, and grow mutually beneficial relationships with specific journalists, bloggers, vloggers, writers, and influencers.

  BUT REMEMBER - DO NOT SPAM THEM – they really do not like it!

A complete PR strategy to help build your personal brand requires a good deal of thought and a lot of commitment. Getting it right, however, should raise your profile in ways that simple branding and advertising won't be able to achieve, by connecting a strong personal brand presence with the overall perception of your brand or business.

At its core, promotion connects your brand to your audience in a multitude of ways, framing both you and your business / brand / employer / industry as a reputable and trustworthy solution to their problems.

In order for you to nurture sustainable professional success, you need to nurture a reputable and positive promotional presence for both you and your brand – as when it comes to consumer perception, the two are one and the same.

All of the aforementioned touchpoints can help you to refine and control the way your personal brand – and subsequently your business – is promoted and presented. Which ones are the most applicable and beneficial to you will depend on your industry and your overall goal.

Make it work for you...

For solopreneurs:

- *Promotion is how you connect and engage with existing clients and how you reach new ones.*
- *It is the best tool you have in your armoury when it comes to client outreach, as it enables you to connect with them in the places where they spend time online.*
- *Your business is your personal brand as a solopreneur, so taking the time to be authentic across all touchpoints is integral to sustainable success.*

For entrepreneurs:

- *The best kind of promotion is that which bridges your personal presence with your business presence across both online and offline touchpoints. As such, your personal promotion needs to support and be coherently in line with your businesses tone of voice and goal.*
- *Entrepreneurs will need to match their target customer with the best platforms on which to promote their business — using metrics and customer avatar personas.*

For intrapreneurs:

- *Promotion is something that can help you to earn a name for yourself as a reliable and responsible professional within your industry - helping to facilitate future opportunities as well as boosting your role and responsibilities.*
- *If you're interested in building a professional profile outside of your work and existing role, promotion can also help you to become an influencer of sorts — for example through a podcast sharing your experiences and expertise, or a blog.*

Bringing it all together...

The role of Perspective, Mindset, and Motivation

This is the part of the book where we fuse together everything that has come before, helping you to finetune not only your personal brand but how it fits within your professional profile as it is now and as it could be over the next 6, 12, and 24 months.

I am a big advocate of short term and long-term goals. A combination of the two is what allows us to celebrate and act positively on a daily basis, while still looking to a future propped up on goals and future opportunities. Recognising the small daily wins is a crucial aspect in all of my client's businesses, as it reignites the passion that drives them forward, and shows them that they are making progress. At the same time, having bigger long term goals keeps them moving forward and striving to be and do better.

This is where perspective and mindset come together to form the ultimate personal brand. Think of it as the power couple behind everything you have achieved, and everything you still want to achieve – whether in your job role, as a solopreneur, or in a new business venture.

"Having perspective about yourself, your strengths and weaknesses is essential in today's world as it enables you to navigate the ever-changing and competitive landscape with confidence and resilience."

With the rise of technology and globalisation, it is essential to understand your capabilities and limitations; leveraging your strengths to create value and differentiate yourself from others.

It's also important to recognise one very specific fact – and it's something it has taken me a LONG time to get my head around. You are not going to be the right fit for everyone – it's impossible. More than that, you don't WANT to try and be the right fit for everyone, because if that's your goal then you've completely overlooked the number one rule of business: to focus on one thing and become an expert in it.

Being a good business person, whether in the role of solopreneur, intrapreneur, or entrepreneur, is about carving out your place in the market or industry you operate in. From there, you can build solid foundations, knowing that you are serving a corner of the market effectively and efficiently, rather than trying to deliver something for everyone.

Having a clear perspective on yourself as a professional helps you to make informed decisions about your career, relationships, and personal growth. It allows you to focus on what you do well, and build a business or a career on that skillset and strength.

It also allows you to delegate tasks that are not your strengths, build better relationships and communicate more effectively with others.

Which leads nicely onto the reason why having a clear perspective on your personal brand is essential for future success - enabling you to understand your unique value proposition and communicate it effectively to your target audience.

Your personal brand is a reflection of your skills, experiences, and values, and having a clear understanding of it can help you stand out in a crowded marketplace, as well as create a compelling narrative that resonates with your audience and inspires them to take action.

Ultimately, having perspective about your personal brand is crucial for creating a strong foundation for future success. And it all comes from a positive mindset and understanding of where you stand now and where you want to be. Of course, that's not to say there aren't challenges you'll come across along the way...

Imposter Syndrome

Have you ever suffered from Imposter Syndrome?
I know I have!

Those moments when you find yourself doubting your abilities.

The times when it becomes impossible to make decisions, with the fear of failure looming over you like some mythical monster.

When you simple can't understand why clients would pay you for a service, or why customers would choose you over a competitor, or why your boss would ever consider you for promotion.

Well, you're not alone...

Imposter Syndrome is a common trait amongst many business owners, senior executives, employees, and solopreneurs.

A 'psychological phenomenon' where individuals doubt their abilities and feel like a fraud, despite accomplishments and qualifications, once imposter syndrome sets in it can be difficult to shake – and is only made worse by the increase in competitors with seemingly cheaper offers or better websites or more stylish logos.

All of this can lead to feelings of anxiety, stress, or fear of being exposed as a fraud – with solopreneurs in particular struggling from this due to their often-isolated workspace and the fact that they operate alone through much of the workday.

Ultimately, this is a fear which may well be holding you back from making progress in your business and achieving your goals.

It can manifest itself in several ways, and it doesn't just affect you.

People who struggle with imposter syndrome are those most likely to struggle with delegating tasks to others, sharing their feelings, seeking feedback or collaborating with others and taking risks.

Having coached and mentored many business owners, senior executives and solopreneurs who suffer from Imposter Syndrome, I would like to share with you some of the advice and guidance I provide (and encourage) to help overcome these challenging thoughts – the first of which is to recognise the signs and work to identify the cause.

The first step in overcoming imposter syndrome is to recognise the signs, such as feelings of self-doubt and fear of failure. It's essential to realise that these feelings are normal, and that you are not alone in experiencing them.

✓ **Reframe Your Thoughts:** Negative thoughts often lead to negative actions.

✓ **Using different strategies, you can reduce (and even eradicate) negative self-talk into positive self-talk.**

Rather than focusing on your weaknesses, focus on your strengths and accomplishments. Most importantly, celebrate your successes and recognise your hard work – through those little wins and short term goals I mentioned earlier.

✓ **Seek Support:** Surround yourself with a supportive network of colleagues, mentors, and friends who can provide guidance and encouragement.

✓ **Feed off the positivity** – and their positive experiences! You could even consider joining a business group or attending conferences to meet like-minded individuals and build a network of support.

✓ **Embrace Failure:** Failure is a natural part of the learning process, but the best way to embrace failure it is to see it as an opportunity for growth and learning.

In reflection ask yourself – have you really 'failed' or was it simply a case of needing more time, experience, or support? Consider your mistakes and use them as a stepping stone for improvement – don't over analyse or dwell to long on these events either!

✓ **Take Action:** Sitting in fear achieves absolutely nothing – agreed?

And yet, so many of us spend hours, days, and even weeks contemplating and berating ourselves for what we have and haven't achieved!

✓ **Take action towards your goals**, despite your fears and doubts. Set small achievable goals and work towards them one step at a time - and don't forget to celebrate your progress along the way – small wins are just as important as the big wins!

✓ **Practice Self-Care:** Taking care of yourself is crucial in overcoming imposter syndrome.

✓ **Make time for self-care activities** such as exercise, meditation, or spending time with loved ones.

Imposter syndrome is real and can hold you back from achieving your full potential in business and life, as you question everything and subconsciously manifest the negative by dwelling on it.

But look at it this way, if you don't believe that you deserve or have worked hard enough towards a promotion at work or a new client contract, then why should anyone else deem you ready or worthy? Imposter syndrome is more likely to get in the way than anything else – and it certainly won't make you feel any more ready to take on the next challenge.

I really hope that the advice I have shared with you helps to realign your negative thoughts and focus more on the positive outcomes.

Remember that success is a journey, and every step towards your goals is a step in the right direction.

Mindset

In this next section, I want to share a handful of the most important things that I have learnt about building a personal brand and enabling that personal brand to shine through in my business life - all without losing the very real 'human' side of what I do.

If you follow me on LinkedIn, you will see that my feed is a combination of personal experiences and announcements, and valuable content and tips for my network of business followers.

Believe it or not, this is completely deliberate. What it does is remind my followers and my network, time and time again, that I am a real person – and that the very human side of my life is at the heart and centre of my brand and my professional offering.

By interjecting personal experiences with high value content, I constantly remind my audience of my professional expertise and knowledge, while inviting them to get to know and connect with me as a person.

Personal branding. You can't beat it.

Here are five ways of letting your personality shine through and around your business, solopreneur venture, or professional role, without losing that integral balance of what's personal and what's professional.

1.   Remember that perfection is an illusion!

Set your goals and keep them realistic.

- Goals are not there to become a whipping-stick when things go wrong, nor are they designed to promote failure!
- Setting a clear (and achievable) direction for your business will keep you focused and heading in the right direction.
- Rome wasn't built in a day - so don't expect instant results for your business empire! Break down large tasks into more manageable bite-size chunks.
- Be kind to yourself! Celebrate ALL the 'wins' — not just the big ones - and do it publicly when you feel comfortable doing so. Let other people join you as you grow and expand.

Perfection is an illusion, so stop striving for it!

2. **Recognise your strengths – and accept your weaknesses!**

- One of my favourite quotes sums this up nicely: *"Growth begins when we begin to accept our weaknesses"* - Jean Vanier.
- Spending too much time worrying about those unreachable goals will hold you back.
- Occasionally we all make mistakes (or stumble across learning curves, as I like to call them). Remember - this is a marathon not a sprint!

3. **Surround yourself with positive like-minded people!**

- Nobody says it better than Mr Einstein: "Stay away from negative people, they have a problem for every solution"
- If you're struggling with self-doubt and a negative mindset, surround yourself with positive people. Feed off their enthusiasm, passion and motivation.
- YOU are your own worst critic! If you're questioning your abilities, talk to someone who can look at what you're doing through fresh eyes.

4. **Keep self-educating!**

- No matter what age or level of experience – education is essential for developing the mind and feeding the soul.
- With the plethora of training courses, webinars and workshops available on the Internet, there's never been a better time to learn something new or develop existing skills. This is particularly pertinent for intrapreneurs who have access to resources which enable them to develop their own professional persona and that which they hold within the company they work for. Find out what training you are able to access and use it!

5.   **Take time out... Have fun and enjoy the journey!**

- Like many, I LOVE what I do, but we can become so engrossed in our daily work that we forget about what's important... getting out from behind the desk and enjoying life! Which is, in the long run, no good for physical or mental health.
- So, take regular time out. Have some fun and enjoy life - it's all part of this rich and exciting journey!

Self-reflection

Self-reflection is the process of examining your own thoughts, emotions, and behaviours in order to gain a deeper understanding of yourself.

It involves asking ourselves questions like:

"What are my strengths and weaknesses?"
"What motivates me?"
"What do I need to improve on?"

Answering these questions can help you to determine the next steps that you need to take to nurture that positive mindset we talked about earlier, and to start cancelling out the imposter syndrome which can become a stain on your progress and success.

Through self-reflection, we gain greater self-awareness and insight into our thoughts, emotions, and behaviours – identifying the small and large things we can do to improve our personal brand for ourselves and for our audience.

Now, this may sound rather scary to some people, which is perfectly natural!

After all, looking at ourselves in the barest sense is tough – and let's face it, most of us tend to spend our working hours 'nose to the grindstone' – rarely giving ourselves chance to think about anything other than the long lists of tasks we need to complete.

When we arrive home, we're too tired to think pretty much about anything – nevermind ourselves. Whilst desperately finding time to speak to our loved ones, we're also scrolling through our social media feeds - squeezing in time to eat - and then binging on Netflix or YouTube, or even catching up on some of the work tasks we didn't complete earlier in the day.

Sound familiar?

I know it definitely used to resonate strongly with me!

However, taking a step back to concentrate on thoughts and emotions, observing them from a more objective perspective, can be a powerful process in changing your beliefs – especially if you are prone to suffering from a negative mindset leading to low self-esteem.

Having suffered from low self-esteem and a negative mindset in the past, I've found self-reflection to be a powerful tool in analysing and challenging my negative thoughts and how they affect my behaviour.

When I do this, I discover a more enlightened and appreciative state of mind and find it easier to acknowledge and be grateful for both the things I have in my life and what I have achieved.

In fact, I wish I had started this practice of self-reflection before I branched out and built my own business, as I think it's truly valuable for intrapreneurs who sometimes struggle to see where their value lies within the larger working organism of a business. Far from becoming lost, this is a way of recognising your role as an integral cog in a larger machine, just like a solopreneur might use this same practice to take a step away and recognise the value they offer to clients and direct customers.

Self-reflection allows us to gain a deeper understanding of ourselves as standalone individuals and as a part of the industry we operate in - identifying our values and our motivations, which in turn help us to make better decisions for our business and for our work-life balance.

Here are some specific ways that self-reflection can benefit us all:

- **Improved Decision Making:** Self-reflection helps us to make more informed and objective decisions.

  When we have a clear understanding of our values, strengths, and weaknesses, we are better equipped to make decisions that align with our goals and values.

- **Increased Self-Awareness:** By reflecting on our thoughts, emotions, and behaviours, we gain a greater understanding of ourselves, our strengths, and our weaknesses.

  This allows us to leverage our strengths and address our weaknesses, which can ultimately lead to greater success in our business.

- **Better Communication:** Effective communication is a crucial component of business management.

  This allows us to leverage our strengths and address our weaknesses, which can ultimately lead to greater success in our business.

  Self-reflection helps us to identify our communication style, as well as any areas where we may need to improve our communication skills.

- **Enhanced Problem Solving:** Reflecting on our past successes and failures helps us to identify patterns and trends in our decision-making and problem-solving approaches.

  This allows us to refine our problem-solving skills and improve our ability to handle challenges in the future.

  It's a crucial tool for personal and professional development, especially when it comes to running a successful business.

With that said, how do we practice self-reflection for our work and general wellbeing?

Here are my 5 steps to help you develop a self-reflection process which works for you:

1. Set Aside Time for Reflection:

Schedule regular time for self-reflection, whether it's daily, weekly, or monthly. This can be as simple as taking a few minutes each day to journal or meditate.

2. Ask Yourself Questions:

Use open-ended questions to prompt self-reflection.

For example:

"What went well in my business this week?"
"What could I have done better?"

"What do I need to focus on next week?"
"What changes can I make in my role or routine that will improve the business for others — both colleagues and customers?"

3. Reflect on Both Successes and Failures:

Don't just focus on what went wrong in your work.

Take time to reflect on your successes as well, consider what you did well and how you can build on those successes.

4. Seek Feedback:

Ask for feedback from trusted colleagues, employees, customers, or other stakeholders.

This can help you to gain an outside perspective and identify areas where you may need to improve.

5. Take Action:

Use your reflections to inform your decision-making and take action to improve your business or your career opportunities.

This may involve setting new goals, making changes to your processes, or seeking out new opportunities.

Incorporating self-reflection into your daily routine enables you to bridge everything I've covered in this book, by encouraging you to take a step away from the everyday tasks and check boxes you cover, and instead consider your position as a professional from an outside perspective. Crucially, we've gone beyond the simple relationship between brand and customer and considered the whole audience – including colleagues and peers as well as competitors and more.

So, what's next?

If you ask me, the best place to start is with a few simple questions:

- Where are you now and what do you want to achieve?

- Is your personal brand something that you already rely heavily on in securing new clients and building new contacts, or are there areas that we have covered in this book which you could work on in order to boost your professional reputation?

- Does the "you" that the world sees match with the "you" that you want your clients or customers to see?

- Is your personal brand bringing in business for your company, while helping you to secure the reputation which will lead to a bright future for you in the workplace?

Whether you're a **solopreneur** monetising your skills and expertise as a marketable service, an **entrepreneur** with ideas for the next big thing, or an **intrapreneur** bringing vision and motivation to the workplace while bolstering your own professional reputation, the personal brand you create is the you that you want to be recognised for by your target audience as a whole.

I hope that this book helps you to see that your personal brand is not a false or dramatised version of you – rather, it is the real you infused with the authenticity that makes people want to engage, connect, and ultimately do business with you.

Without my personal brand, I'm just another guy selling a book.

And there must be a reason you picked **this** book up...

Useful Resources

Welcome to the 'Useful Resources' section of this book – rather like a dictionary but better and certainly more useful for all you 'preneurs', regardless of your position!

Hopefully by now, you understand the importance of marketing and sales in growing your personal brand. However, navigating the ever-evolving world of marketing and sales can be overwhelming, especially if you are new to the field. That's why I have compiled a list of some of the most useful resources available to help you improve your strategy and drive results. From content creation to email marketing, SEO to social media management, and everything in between, we have identified some of the best tools and platforms to help you optimize your marketing efforts and grow your business.

Whether you're looking to streamline your workflow, improve your search engine rankings, or engage with your audience on social media, this section provides you with a comprehensive overview of the most popular and effective marketing and sales resources available today.

So, let's dive in and explore the tools that can help take your business to the next level!

Website creation platforms:

- **Kajabi** is an all-in-one platform designed for entrepreneurs and small businesses to create and sell online courses, membership sites, and digital products. It offers various features such as website design, email marketing, sales funnels, and analytics to help businesses create and manage their digital content. This is the platform I've created my business in and can highly recommend.

- **WordPress** is an open-source content management system (CMS) used to build websites and blogs. It offers a wide range of customisable themes, plugins, and features that allow businesses to create and manage their online presence easily. WordPress is widely used and has a large community of developers creating additional features and themes.

- **Wix** is a cloud-based website builder that allows businesses to create and host websites without any coding knowledge. It offers a drag-and-drop editor and a variety of templates, making it easy to create a professional-looking website quickly.

- **Thinkific** is an online course platform designed for businesses to create, sell, and deliver online courses. It offers features such as website design, course creation tools, and student management tools to help businesses create and manage their digital courses.

- **Squarespace** is a website builder that allows businesses to create and host websites with pre-designed templates and a drag-and-drop editor. It offers features such as website design, e-commerce tools, and blogging tools to help businesses create a professional online presence.

Content creation tools – design:

- **Canva** is a web-based graphic design tool that allows businesses to create professional-looking designs such as social media graphics, presentations, flyers, and posters. It offers a wide range of templates, images, and design elements that users can customize to suit their needs. Canva also has a free plan with basic features and a paid plan with more advanced features.

- **Adobe Creative Cloud** is a suite of software tools designed for graphic design, video editing, web development, and photography. It includes popular applications such as Photoshop, Illustrator, InDesign, and Premiere Pro. Adobe Creative Cloud is widely used by professionals and offers a vast range of features for creating and managing digital content.

- **Microsoft Designer** is a web-based graphic design tool that allows businesses to create designs for social media, presentations, and other digital media. It offers a range of templates, images, and design elements that users can customise to suit their needs. Microsoft Designer is free and integrated with Microsoft Office 365.

- **Genial.ly** is a web-based interactive content creation tool that allows businesses to create and share interactive content such as presentations, infographics, and quizzes. It offers a range of templates, images, and design elements that users can customise to suit their needs. Genial.ly also offers analytics and collaboration features to help businesses manage their interactive content.

- **Designrr** is a web-based eBook creation tool that allows businesses to create and publish eBooks, reports, and whitepapers. It offers a range of templates, images, and design elements that users can customize to suit their needs. Designrr also offers collaboration features and integrations with popular publishing platforms such as Kindle and iBooks.

Content creation tools – copywriting:

- **ChatGPT** is an AI-powered chatbot that can assist businesses with a wide range of tasks, including copywriting. ChatGPT can generate content for businesses such as social media posts, product descriptions, and email marketing campaigns. It is designed to mimic human conversation and can be customized to suit a business's needs.

- **Copy.ai** is an AI-powered copywriting tool that can help businesses create compelling content such as social media posts, blog articles, and product descriptions. It offers a range of templates and customization options to help businesses generate content quickly and easily.

- **Jasper** is a web-based writing assistant that helps businesses write better content by providing suggestions for grammar, style, and tone. It uses AI to analyse text and offers feedback on sentence structure, word choice, and readability. Jasper can be integrated with popular writing tools such as Google Docs and Microsoft Word.

- **Grammarly** is a writing assistant that helps businesses improve their writing by providing suggestions for grammar, spelling, and style. It offers a web-based editor and browser extension that can be used to check emails, social media posts, and other digital content. Grammarly also provides feedback on sentence structure, tone, and readability.

Content creation tools – stock images:

- **Unsplash** is a free online image library that offers a wide range of high-quality photographs and graphics. The images on Unsplash are contributed by a community of photographers and can be used for commercial and non-commercial purposes without attribution.

- **Pexels** is a free online image library that offers a range of high-quality photographs and videos. The images on Pexels are contributed by a community of photographers and can be used for commercial and non-commercial purposes without attribution.

- **Pixabay** is a free online image library that offers a wide range of photographs, illustrations, and vector graphics. The images on Pixabay can be used for commercial and non-commercial purposes without attribution.

- **Shutterstock** is a paid online image library that offers a vast selection of high-quality photographs, illustrations, and videos. It offers a range of pricing options depending on the number of images needed and how they will be used. Shutterstock also offers editorial and music content for licensing.

- **Gratisography** is a free online image library that offers a range of quirky and whimsical photographs. The images on Gratisography are taken by photographer Ryan McGuire and can be used for commercial and non-commercial purposes without attribution.

Content creation tools – video:

- **Lumen5** is a web-based video production tool that allows businesses to create short videos for social media, marketing, and other purposes. It uses AI to turn blog articles or text into videos by matching text with relevant images and video clips. Lumen5 also offers customisation options, such as adding music and text overlays.

- **Kapwing** is a web-based video editing tool that allows businesses to create and edit videos for social media, marketing, and other purposes. It offers a range of editing features, such as adding text, filters, and animations, and can be used to create videos from scratch or edit existing footage.

- **Giphy** is a web-based platform that allows businesses to create and share animated GIFs and short videos. It offers a range of tools for creating and customising GIFs, such as adding text and stickers, and can be used to create content for social media, messaging, and other purposes.

- **InVideo** is a cloud-based video creation platform that allows users to create high-quality videos for marketing, social media, and other purposes without the need for professional video editing experience. The platform offers a range of tools and features, such as text-to-video, video editing tools, and automated voiceovers, to make the video creation process more straightforward and efficient.

- **Loom** is a web-based screen recording tool that allows businesses to create and share videos for presentations, tutorials, and other purposes. It offers a range of recording options, such as recording the screen, webcam, or both, and can be used to create videos quickly and easily. Loom also offers editing and sharing features to help businesses manage their video content.

Content creation tools – podcast:

- **Audacity** is a free and open-source audio editing software that allows businesses to record and edit podcast audio. It offers a range of features such as multi-track recording, editing, and audio effects to help businesses create high-quality audio content.

- **Streamyard** is a web-based live streaming platform that allows businesses to record and broadcast podcasts live on various social media platforms. It offers features such as multi-camera support, screen sharing, and branding options to help businesses create a professional-looking podcast.

- **Buzzsprout** is a web-based podcast hosting platform that allows businesses to upload, host, and distribute their podcast audio to various platforms such as Apple Podcasts, Spotify, and Google Podcasts. It offers a range of features such as analytics, promotional tools, and website integration to help businesses manage and grow their podcast audience.

- **Riverside.fm** is a web-based podcast recording platform that allows businesses to record high-quality audio and video podcasts remotely. It offers features such as automatic audio and video syncing, multi-track recording, and live streaming to help businesses create professional-quality podcast content.

- **Anchor.fm** is a web-based podcast creation and distribution platform that allows businesses to record and edit podcasts and distribute them to various platforms such as Apple Podcasts, Spotify, and Google Podcasts. It offers a range of features such as recording and editing tools, music and sound effects libraries, and analytics to help businesses create and grow their podcast audience.

Content creation tools – workflow and collaboration:

- **Trello** is a web-based project management tool that allows businesses to organise and prioritise tasks and projects. It offers a simple, user-friendly interface with boards, lists, and cards to help businesses keep track of progress and deadlines. Trello also offers collaboration and communication features to help teams work together more efficiently.

- **Google Workspace** (formerly G Suite) is a suite of web-based productivity tools designed for businesses. It includes applications such as Gmail, Google Drive, Google Docs, and Google Calendar, and offers a range of features such as email, document collaboration, and project management.

- **Monday** is a web-based project management and team collaboration tool that allows businesses to manage projects and tasks more efficiently. It offers features such as customisable workflows, automations, and integrations with other tools to help businesses streamline their work processes.

- **Hive** is a web-based project management and collaboration tool that allows businesses to manage tasks, projects, and team communication in one platform. It offers features such as customisable project templates, time tracking, and resource management to help businesses optimise their workflow.

- **Miro** is a web-based collaboration and whiteboard tool that allows businesses to collaborate and brainstorm ideas visually. It offers a range of features such as virtual whiteboards, templates, and collaboration tools to help businesses work together more effectively. Miro also offers integrations with other tools such as Trello and Slack.

Social media management tools:

- **Buffer** is a web-based social media management tool that allows businesses to schedule and publish posts on various social media platforms, such as Facebook, Twitter, LinkedIn, and Instagram. It offers features such as post scheduling, analytics, and team collaboration to help businesses manage their social media presence.

- **Hootsuite** is a web-based social media management tool that allows businesses to manage and schedule posts on various social media platforms. It offers features such as post scheduling, analytics, and social listening to help businesses monitor and engage with their audience on social media.

- **Loomly** is a web-based social media management tool that allows businesses to create, schedule, and publish posts on various social media platforms. It offers features such as post suggestions, post preview, and analytics to help businesses optimise their social media content.

- **Sprout Social** is a web-based social media management and optimisation tool that allows businesses to manage their social media presence and engage with their audience. It offers features such as post scheduling, analytics, social listening, and automation to help businesses streamline their social media workflow.

- **Feedly** is a web-based content aggregation and curation tool that allows businesses to discover and share content on various social media platforms. It offers features such as RSS feed integration, content suggestions, and content categorisation to help businesses find and share relevant content with their audience.

Email marketing tools:

- **MailChimp** is a web-based email marketing tool that allows businesses to create, send, and track email campaigns. It offers features such as email automation, segmentation, and analytics to help businesses optimize their email marketing efforts.

- **ActiveCampaign** is a web-based email marketing and automation tool that allows businesses to create and send personalized emails to their audience. It offers features such as automation workflows, CRM integration, and analytics to help businesses optimize their email marketing and sales efforts.

- **MailerLite** is a web-based email marketing tool that allows businesses to create and send email campaigns. It offers features such as automation workflows, landing pages, and analytics to help businesses optimize their email marketing efforts.

- **GetResponse** is a web-based email marketing tool that allows businesses to create and send email campaigns. It offers features such as automation workflows, landing pages, and analytics to help businesses optimize their email marketing efforts. GetResponse also offers webinar marketing and e-commerce tools.

- **HubSpot Email Marketing** is a web-based email marketing tool that allows businesses to create and send email campaigns. It offers features such as automation workflows, personalisation, and analytics to help businesses optimise their email marketing efforts.

HubSpot Email Marketing is integrated with HubSpot's CRM and marketing tools, allowing businesses to manage their entire marketing and sales funnel in one platform.

Search Engine Optimisation (SEO) tools:

- **Semrush** is a web-based SEO tool that allows businesses to analyse their website's search engine performance and optimise their SEO strategy. It offers features such as keyword research, competitor analysis, backlink analysis, and site audit to help businesses improve their search engine rankings.

- **Ubersuggest** is a web-based SEO tool that allows businesses to analyse their website's search engine performance and identify opportunities for optimisation. It offers features such as keyword research, site audit, and competitor analysis to help businesses improve their search engine rankings.

- **Ahrefs** is a web-based SEO tool that allows businesses to analyse their website's search engine performance and optimize their SEO strategy. It offers features such as keyword research, backlink analysis, and site audit to help businesses improve their search engine rankings and drive traffic to their website.

- **Google Search Console** and **Google Analytics** are web-based tools provided by Google that allow businesses to monitor and analyse their website's search engine performance and traffic. Google Search Console provides insights into how Google crawls and indexes your website, while Google Analytics provides insights into website traffic, user behaviour, and conversion tracking.

- **Moz** is a web-based SEO tool that allows businesses to analyse their website's search engine performance and optimise their SEO strategy. It offers features such as keyword research, site audit, and link building tools to help businesses improve their search engine rankings and drive traffic to their website. Moz also provides a range of educational resources and SEO best practices to help businesses stay up-to-date with the latest SEO trends.

Public Relations (PR) tools:

- **Cision** is a web-based PR tool that allows businesses to manage their media outreach and track their PR efforts. It offers features such as media monitoring, journalist databases, and media outreach tools to help businesses build relationships with journalists and secure media coverage.

- **Mention** is a web-based PR tool that allows businesses to monitor and track their brand mentions on social media and other online platforms. It offers features such as real-time alerts, sentiment analysis, and competitor tracking to help businesses manage their online reputation.

- **PR Web** releases and reach journalists and media outlets. It offers features such as distribution to major news outlets, analytics, and social media sharing to help businesses increase their visibility and reach.

- **BuzzStream** is a web-based PR tool that allows businesses to manage their outreach campaigns and build relationships with influencers and journalists. It offers features such as contact management, email tracking, and analytics to help businesses streamline their outreach efforts.

- **Google Alerts** is a free web-based tool that allows businesses to monitor and track their brand mentions and relevant topics on the web. It offers features such as email alerts and real-time notifications to help businesses stay up to date with the latest news and trends in their industry.

Presentation tools:

- **Zoom** is a web-based video conferencing tool that allows businesses to conduct webinars, online meetings, and virtual events. It offers features such as screen sharing, recording, and live streaming to help businesses engage with their audience remotely.

- **Webinar Ninja** is a web-based webinar platform that allows businesses to create and host webinars. It offers features such as customizable landing pages, email automation, and analytics to help businesses optimize their webinar strategy and generate leads.

- **Prezi** is a web-based presentation tool that allows businesses to create dynamic and engaging presentations. It offers features such as non-linear presentations, animations, and multimedia integration to help businesses make their presentations more memorable and impactful.

- **Beautiful.ai** is a web-based presentation tool that allows businesses to create professional-looking presentations quickly and easily. It offers features such as smart templates, design automation, and collaboration tools to help businesses create visually appealing presentations without design skills.

- **Slidebean** is a web-based presentation tool that allows businesses to create professional-looking presentations quickly and easily. It offers features such as AI-powered design suggestions, real-time collaboration, and analytics to help businesses create effective presentations and track their performance.

Please help me encourage more people to master their 5-P-Preneur Blueprint...

Review my book and earn a reward!

I've created a special companion workbook, designed to accompany your "5-P Preneur" journey - helping and guiding you to implement the concepts, models and principles I have discussed in this book.

To receive a free digital copy of my 5-P-Preneur workbook, all I request is a review of my book - Infectious - on whatever website you purchased it from.

Email a copy of your review (via a link or screenshot) to simon@marketingskillsacademy.co.uk and I'll reply attaching my 5-P-Preneur Blueprint wordbook!